A FIGHTER COMMAND STATION AT WAR

A Photographic Record of RAF Westhampnett
from The Battle of Britain to D-Day and Beyond

This book is dedicated to the memory of those pilots and personnel who served,
and sometimes made the ultimate sacrifice,
whilst flying from or were based at RAF Westhampnett.

A FIGHTER COMMAND STATION AT WAR

A Photographic Record of RAF Westhampnett
from The Battle of Britain to D-Day and Beyond

Mark Hillier

Foreword by The Earl of March and Kinrara

A FIGHTER COMMAND STATION AT WAR
A Photographic Record of RAF Westhampnett from the Battle of Britain to D-Day and Beyond

This edition published in 2015 by Frontline Books,
an imprint of Pen & Sword Books Ltd,
47 Church Street, Barnsley, S. Yorkshire, S70 2AS.

ISBN: 978-1-47384-468-1

CIP data records for this title are available from the British Library

Printed and bound by CPI Group (UK) Ltd, Croydon, CR0 4YY
Typeset in 9/11 point Palatino

For more information on our books, please email: info@frontline-books.com,
write to us at the above address, or visit:
www.frontline-books.com

CONTENTS

FOREWORD

The history of Westhampnett has always interested me, not just because it's on the Goodwood estate, but because it was from the perimeter roads of the aerodrome that my Grandfather created the motor circuit back in 1948. So I am delighted to be writing the Foreword for a book that records, and preserves, the history of the place.

I have so many happy childhood memories of the Easter Monday race meetings, watching with my Grandfather in his little caravan by the chicane and meeting all the famous drivers. This was where my passion for motor racing began, where the inspiration to revive the circuit came from in 1998, and why we stage the Goodwood Revival every year.

The Revival is not simply a race meeting, it's also a celebration of both the pilots and the aircraft that flew from here in the Second World War. Mark Hillier's finely detailed book reminds us of Westhampnett's vital role as a frontline wartime base, so when the Spitfires, Hurricanes and Mustangs fly here each September we remember the skill and bravery of the men who went into those dogfights with so little training.

Until I looked at the remarkable photographs collected for *A Fighter Command Station at War*, I hadn't fully appreciated the importance of RAF Westhampnett in some of the biggest air battles of the war. Many of the pilots who fly from Goodwood aerodrome today feel that sense of history,

aware that they are using pretty much the same grass runways used by the men who went to the Dieppe Raid, the D-Day landings, and the Battle of Normandy.

It was, I learnt, a truly international community as well, with pilots from America, Canada, France, Poland, New Zealand and Belgium. Apparently the locals weren't too keen on the noise of the Typhoons with their huge Napier Sabre engines. Thankfully, things are a lot quieter at our aerodrome these days.

Immediately after the war, as the country gradually got back on its feet, the sport of motor racing needed a new home and aerodromes were the perfect place to start. It was an RAF fighter pilot, Tony Gaze, who alerted my Grandfather to Westhampnett's potential as a circuit and it's thanks to him that we have the historic track that we still use to this day.

This book takes us back in time and I hope you will enjoy the journey as much as I did. The skill and courage of the Westhampnett pilots must never be forgotten.

Earl of March and Kinrara
Goodwood, 2015

A PILOT'S PERSPECTIVE

My final appointment in the Royal Navy was Commanding Officer of the Royal Navy Historic Flight, which for me was a marvelous way to end thirty-seven years as a Fleet Air Arm pilot. After retirement from the Royal Navy, I was fortunate to become involved with the Boultbee Flight Academy, based at Goodwood Aerodrome, as a flying instructor. The Academy was formed to teach modern pilots to fly the Spitfire. Consequently, it has a fleet of vintage aircraft to replicate the process a Second World War pilot would have undertaken before becoming operational in a Spitfire. Operating from the former RAF Westhampnett adds a huge amount to that experience as the fabric of the airfield has changed very little since the 1940s.

The link between the Fleet Air Arm and RAF Westhampnett is very strong. The last military flying unit based at the aerodrome was 787 Naval Air Fighting Development Unit. It operated Barracudas, Avengers and Wildcats before handing the airfield back to the Goodwood Estate in 1946. Many Fleet Air Arm pilots served with the RAF during the Battle of Britain and afterwards. Some flew from Westhampnett, including Colin "Hoppy" Hodgkinson and Sub Lieutenant Francis Alan Smith RN, the later killed during the Battle of Britain.

Flying from Goodwood today has changed very little since it was created on little more than farmland in the Second World War. The airfield still has grass runways and becomes soft and boggy during the winter months after a good downpour.

The opportunity to make a low pass over Chichester Cathedral in a Spitfire on a Sunday morning is long gone, but once in the air and you have filtered out the urban sprawl, the scene from the cockpit is exactly the same as 1940; Selsey Bill to the south, Isle of Wight and Portsmouth to the West, and the South Downs to the East. It does not take much imagination, especially when you are sat in a Spitfire, to visualize what it must have been like flying in that piece of airspace during the war.

The many visitors who come to fly in the Boultbee Flight Academy's Spitfire TR9 (a two-seat variant) often ask about the history of Goodwood Aerodrome. Whilst it is always a pleasure to recount the history of the place, Mark Hillier's book provides all the answers for us and gives a unique and detailed insight into the actual life of "A Fighter Command Station at War".

Lieutenant Commander Mike Abbey MBE, MSc, RN
Goodwood, 2015

INTRODUCTION

The sky is blue and the wind light as I pull the aircraft out for its pre-flight inspection, eager in anticipation of another flight over the beautiful countryside of West Sussex and the South Downs.

I climb in and perform my cockpit checks. I prime the engine, shout 'clear prop' and push the starter. The engine barks in to life and I gently allow it to warm up prior to taxiing to the holding point. With pre-take-off checks done, I take a quick look at the wind direction whilst I line up. Making sure the tail wheel is straight, I push the power on and inch the stick gently forwards to get the tail up. I nudge the right rudder to correct the swing as I charge down the runway. I am airborne at 75mph and climbing in to the wild blue yonder in a 1943 Boeing Stearman biplane.

No German fighters to watch out for today, just a quick local trip. I take the Stearman and slip the surly bonds of earth, carefree!

Having flown from Goodwood for a number of years, I had known for a while that the airfield's origins date back to the Second World War. For many years I did not bother to research its history any further, or seek to find out what squadrons had been based there. That interest was sparked after being asked to write an article on 602 Squadron for a magazine. For many months I scoured the bookshelves and libraries for references to RAF Westhampnett and slowly I managed to uncover its history.

Now as I fly out of the circuit and look back over my shoulder, I can almost imagine seeing Spitfires and hearing Merlins roar. I can almost visualise 602 (City of Glasgow) Squadron's 'A' Flight getting airborne when RAF Westhampnett was caught in the thick of the action on 16 August 1940, only to then be confronted by skies full of Junkers Ju 87s and Messerschmitt Bf 109s, the German dive bombers doing their utmost to destroy nearby RAF Tangmere.

As I continued with my research I found out that 129 (Mysore) Squadron, which had been based at the airfield, had been involved in the infamous Channel Dash operation in 1942. Its Spitfires flew from Westhampnett to attack *Scharnhorst* and *Gneisenau* as the warships tried to escape up the English Channel to the safety of German-held ports.

The airfield also played host to the first American squadrons in the European Theatre, in particular the 309th Fighter Squadron, which gave air support to the Dieppe raid, of that same year.

As I uncovered more information, and corresponded with a number of the surviving air and groundcrew, it became apparent that Westhampnett had played a significant role as a front line station during the Battle of Britain and after, right through to providing air support for the D-Day landings in 1944 and during Operation *Market Garden*, the airborne landings at Arnhem.

Today the former RAF station is a hive of general aviation activity with few clues left of its wartime pedigree. The airfield grew from its humble beginnings as an emergency landing ground for RAF Tangmere to a thriving RAF station, often with three or four resident squadrons at any one time. Towards the end of its service use, RAF Westhampnett encompassed the surrounding villages and farms and one of its runways extended outside the airfield boundaries as we currently know them.

RAF Westhampnett was home to French, Canadian, American, Polish, New Zealand, and Belgian squadrons, also both RAF and Fleet Air Arm units. The station resounded to the noise of Hurricanes, Spitfires, Typhoons, Tempests, Mustangs, Barracudas, Avengers and Tigercats, amongst many others – although the local residents were not too keen on the noise produced by the Typhoon with its twenty-four cylinder Napier Sabre engine!

Many young pilots took off from Westhampnett during the war, knowing full well that it might be the last time they would see home. A large number were shot down or suffered mechanical failure and were taken prisoner, to be interned for the rest of the war. For some, their final views of Britain would have included the airfield and nearby Chichester cathedral as they departed south on operations, never to return.

This book follows the growth and changes that Westhampnett experienced throughout the war and charts the main actions that squadrons were involved in. Some of the many photographs have not been published before; others had previously been incorrectly labelled as depicting Tangmere. Fortunately, the backdrop of the South Downs to the north of Goodwood, the distinctive tree line on the airfield's eastern boundary, or the unusual accommodation erected at the time (and clearly shown on wartime airfield maps) make it easier to positively identify these images.

In the course of my research (some of which featured in an earlier publication on the airfield) I have scoured squadron records, corresponded with pilots and groundcrew who served at RAF Westhampnett, collected new photographs and gathered together a wide selection of first-hand accounts. It has not been possible, however, to represent in images all of the forty-six squadrons that passed through the station between 1940 and 1946.

At the same time, I have also spoken to people who talk of landing trials of de Havilland Mosquitoes which were undertaken at Westhampnett during 1944. Locating corroborating evidence or images for these accounts has proven impossible, though it would seem that the runways were not suitable for fully-laden aircraft of this size and no Mosquito squadrons were permanently based there.

There are, no doubt, still photographs, diaries and log books out there that will reveal which other units may have operated from Westhampnett. For now, however, this publication puts this important fighter station back on the historical map.

Mark Hillier
Fontwell, 2015

ACKNOWLEDGEMENTS

There have been many people involved in researching and producing this book, much of which is based on a previous publication. In particular I must thank Dieter Sinanan and Greg Percival for allowing me to quote text from this book.

I must thank my wife and daughter for their understanding in allowing me to complete another project. Also Martin Mace who encouraged me to re-explore the Westhampnett story further. In no particular order, the following individuals (many of whom have now sadly passed away) or organisations have all been of much help during the research for, and writing of, this book: Sergeant John Anderson 610 Squadron; Squadron Leader Doug Brown MID; Warrant Officer David Denchfield; Mary Denton; Lieutenant General Baron Michael Donnet CVO DFC; Sergeant Peter Graham; Flying Officer A. Herbst; Wing Commander Bob Middlemiss DFC; Flight Lieutenant Nigel Rose; Fight Sergeant Ray Sherk; Flight Lieutenant Sir Alan Smith DFC & Bar; Flight Lieutenant John Thompson; Flight Sergeant F. Wheeler DFC; Nancy Strawn Adams; English Heritage NMR; Serge Bonge; Steve Brew; Hamish Brown; David Coxon; Nigel Denchfield; Mark Gibb, Imperial War Museum; Denis Kucera; Michael Lewis and the 610 (County of Chester) Squadron Association; RAF Museum Hendon; 602 Squadron Museum; Kevin Moffat; Steve Scrunnels; Peter Sikora; Tangmere Military Aviation Museum; Chris Thomas; Bill Whalen; Andy Saunders; John Grehan; and Rob Wildeboer.

Where possible we have tried to gain copyright permission for all material contained within this book. If any credits have been misappropriated or incorrectly stated the author will ensure that any future publications are corrected.

1

IN THE BEGINNING

If you speak to anyone about motor racing, horse racing or golf in West Sussex, then Goodwood will invariably be on the tip of their tongue – and rightly so. It was, of course, also an operational airfield during the Second World War.

RAF Goodwood, or RAF Woodcote as it was described in an account by a member of 610 (County of Chester) Squadron's groundcrew in 1941, later became known by all as RAF Westhampnett, as is borne out by entries in pilots' log books of the period. Units from the airfield played a vital part in many of the major operations of the Second World War, though few are aware of its important role. Even fewer are aware of a pre-war link with aviation through the 9th Duke of Richmond.

Frederick Charles Gordon Lennox, the 9th Duke of Richmond, Lennox, Gordon and Aubigny (1904-1989), had been a keen aviator. He not only designed and flew his own aircraft, but developed his own flying field to the south of Goodwood House, complete with a thatched hangar to house his aircraft. Along with Edmund Hordern, a former test pilot, in 1937 the 9th Duke of Richmond also co-founded Hordern-Richmond Aircraft Ltd.

The land that the current Goodwood airfield was constructed on was once a collection of fields belonging to the Goodwood Estate located to the south-west of the Duke's own airfield. As the threat of war grew, this area of flat land was requisitioned by the Air Ministry. The intention at the time had not been to construct a fully operational airfield, rather an emergency landing ground for nearby RAF Tangmere.

With its origins dating back to around 1916, Tangmere played a key role in the Battle of Britain as a Sector (or controlling) Station in 11 Group's 'A' Sector. It served on the front line throughout the war, remaining an important RAF station through to 1967.

In 1938, RAF Goodwood was literally a field with no purpose-built facilities other than a windsock. However, the status of the airfield changed just prior to the Battle of Britain when it was upgraded to serve as a satellite airfield of Tangmere and grass runways were laid out. Only then did some basic facilities start to appear, amongst which was a Watch Office. Early aerial photographs show that the RAF went to some lengths to camouflage the airfield by trying to create fake hedges and field boundaries using tar on the ground to break up the shape and confuse prying *Luftwaffe* eyes.

Nearly all of the pilots and groundcrew who have contributed their stories during the research for this book, and a previous publication, commented on the lack of facilities throughout the early stages of the war.[1] Most commonly mentioned was the issue of having to maintain the aircraft in the open and airmen sleeping in tented accommodation – although the officers were initially billeted in relatively luxurious surroundings, initially at Woodcote Farm then Shopwyke House.

The two cottages that stood within the airfield boundary were quickly put to good use, as were many surrounding buildings, accommodating, for example, the NCO pilots and cooking/messing facilities. By the time 145 Squadron left Westhampnett mid-way through the Battle of Britain, at least two flight huts had been constructed. That for 'A' Flight was located by the northernmost cottage on the airfield opposite Woodcote Farm and along the Lavant Straight of the racecourse. 'B' Flight, on the other hand, was situated by the Vitrae Café, or the old control tower, along the eastern boundary following the road back to Chichester.

Previous page: The 9th Duke of Richmond's hangar was situated across the road to the north of Woodcote Farm. This was the earliest airfield at Goodwood. Later on, after occupation of the adjacent land by the RAF in 1940, the hangar was used by various members of groundcrew and associated personnel as accommodation. (The Goodwood Collection)

Opposite: A recent aerial view of Goodwood airfield, the former RAF Westhampnett, looking from the south-east. (Historic Military Press)

In the winter of 1940-1941, the airfield was badly waterlogged and the decision was made to put in a perimeter track as well as erect blister hangars so that maintenance did not have to be carried out in the open. Even when 610 (County of Chester) Squadron moved in during the latter part of 1940, aircraft were still taken through gaps in the hedges to an adjacent barn to be maintained!

At this stage of the war accommodation was still at a premium and the Kennels, a grand building to the north of the field which was owned by the Duke, and nearly all of the surrounding farm buildings, including Woodcote Farm, were used to accommodate airmen. Some of the groundcrew were even installed in the racecourse grandstand and, according to Squadron Leader A.V.R. 'Sandy' Johnstone, the Commanding Officer of 602 (City of Glasgow) Squadron, the club house of the Golf Course was also commandeered. There is still some debate about when the first perimeter track was installed and pilots who were stationed at the airfield in 1941-1942 say they do not recall such a feature at this time. There exists, however, a photograph of the airfield which was taken by the Air Ministry in 1941, that clearly shows the presence of a perimeter road or track, as well as hard standings, albeit that they appear to be very basic in nature.

By the end of the war, RAF Westhampnett had been extensively developed and the site encompassed many of the surrounding villages. It had been home to at least forty-six squadrons and sub-units, some of these were based at the airfield more than once, as well as many thousands of service personnel.

2

THE BATTLE OF BRITAIN

After the fall of France in 1940, the RAF was hard pushed to replenish the crippling losses sustained before and during the evacuation effort. It was fortunate that Fighter Command had resisted calls to deploy more fighter resources in the struggle to save France. A German invasion of the United Kingdom was considered by many to be inevitable, but could only be achieved if the *Luftwaffe* could control the skies during the crossing of the Channel.

This was recognized by Adolf Galland, the *Geschwaderkommodore* of *Jagdgeschwader 26* (*JG 26*), who insisted on "the achievement of air supremacy as a preliminary to the invasion". The *Luftwaffe*'s plan was to destroy Britain's air defences on the ground and in the air prior to their invasion, code-named Operation *Sealion*. *Reichsmarschall* Hermann Göring, the Commander-in-Chief of the *Luftwaffe*, initially ordered his aircrew to target British supply convoys and ports, radar stations and planned landing areas on the South Coast of England. The odds seemed overwhelming with 640 British fighters opposing 2,600 enemy fighters and bombers.

Tuesday, 13 August 1940, a day that came to be known as *Adlertag* ('Eagle Day'), was the first day of *Unternehmen Adlerangriff* (Operation *Eagle Attack*), the *Luftwaffe*'s offensive which was intended to destroy the RAF. It opened with the first mass strikes on the RAF's airfields. Though the Germans failed to break Fighter Command, the attacks persisted. As the weeks rolled on, night raiders intensified the pressure on already stretched defences as serviceable aircraft decreased in number and casualties rose.

Air Chief Marshal Hugh Dowding, the head of Fighter Command, and 11 Group's commander, Air Vice Marshal Keith Park, resisted the call for the fighters to be withdrawn north of the Thames, for fear of leaving the South Coast vulnerable to the enemy invasion fleet that was reportedly mustering on the opposite side of the Channel.

On 7 September 1940, in a dramatic change of tactics, the *Luftwaffe* began bombing London, inadvertently giving respite to the airfields and radar stations. This allowed the RAF to continue its dogged resistance despite the losses, fatigue and a shortage of pilots.

With the Battle of Britain raging above, RAF Westhampnett had become involved as Fighter Command verged on the brink of total collapse. The airfield was now at the forefront of 11 Group's battle to defeat the *Luftwaffe*.

The first squadron to find a home at Westhampnett, by then a formal satellite of the key Sector Station of RAF Tangmere, was 145 Squadron. Formed at Croydon in 1939 and equipped with Bristol Blenheims, the squadron had subsequently converted to Hawker Hurricane Mk.Is in March 1940. It moved to RAF Tangmere on 10 May 1940, though 'A' Flight was despatched to Abbeville to assist in the Battle of France on 18 May 1940.

It was on 23 July 1940 that 145 Squadron moved to Westhampnett.[1] It was led by Squadron Leader John Peel, who had taken command only days earlier. Peel had already seen action and had been shot down whilst operating from Tangmere; he was forced to ditch in the Channel off Selsey Bill on 11 July whilst flying Hurricane P3400 and was rescued by the local

---

Previous page: Taken in June 1940, this is one of the earliest photographs of RAF personnel at Westhampnett. Known as the Headquarters Flight, these men were posted in from nearby Tangmere to help establish the airfield. The building behind went on to serve as the station armoury and can still be seen by visitors to Goodwood today. (Author's Collection)

Opposite: The 145 Squadron Hurricane which, coded 'SO-K', was flown by Flight Lieutenant Adrian Hope Boyd. Note the blister adaption to the standard Hurricane cockpit which had been requested by Boyd to enable better visibility. (ww2images.com)

This page: A close-up view of Boyd's aircraft. It is parked near the eastern boundary at Westhampnett, with straps hanging out of the cockpit. Note the panel which has been removed for servicing. (Andrew Thomas)

Opposite: Hurricane 'SO-K' landing at Westhampnett from the direction of Goodwood. Note the 450 gallon fuel bowser by the hedge. (Tangmere Military Aviation Museum)

Boyd achieved his first victory in the Battle of France, continuing his successes to be awarded the DFC in June 1940. The aircraft he flew at Westhampnett was Hurricane Mk.I P3221. Coded SO-K, this aircraft had a blister hood fitted. As this was not an approved modification Boyd was soon ordered to standardise his machine.

Flight Lieutenant Boyd also had a somewhat unusual hobby, as Aircraftman Eric Marsden once described: "Boyd had a fascination with German ammunition and would put them in a fitter's bench and take them apart. If he could not get them apart he would hacksaw them apart – [on one occasion] this one started smoking, he told Peter Parrott to go and get a kettle and pour water on it."[3]

Marsden was one of those who, posted to RAF Westhampnett in its early days, recalled how the accommodation was extremely basic: "We found there was no provision for us at all; there were three unfinished Nissen huts and little else and this was about the middle of July 1940. The dining hall was the wagon shed of the farm, rough tables only and that dining room was for everyone, pilots and ground crew alike. There were birds in the rafters and spiders dropping down into the food.

"What was supposed to be our billets were brick huts with corrugated roofs with windows and doors either end. We painted the windows black for the blackout, but there was no power. The concrete floors were set but not yet dry; no bed boards, no anything. The washing facilities was the existing farm trough in the field with two boards across it, six zinc basins resting on the planks.

"We were told to get on with it. At that time we had ground sheets or capes, the chaps put groundsheets down and put their bedding on top. We looked in the hedge and pulled out fence boards and bricks to make makeshift beds."[4]

From the moment that 145 Squadron arrived at Westhampnett the squadron flew regular patrols, sometimes as many as five a day, but did not encounter the enemy until 27 July. On this date, Flight Lieutenant Boyd

lifeboat.[2] Peel was awarded the Distinguished Flying Cross on 13 August 1940, the day before 145 Squadron departed Westhampnett for a well-earned rest.

Serving under Peel in 145 Squadron were a number of men who would go on to become distinguished pilots in their own right – men such as Peter Parrott and Adrian Hope Boyd, a pre-war pilot who was posted to the squadron when it was still operating Bristol Blenheims at Croydon.

and Pilot Officer James Storrar sighted a dogfight in progress over the Needles and joined in. Whilst Storrar shot down a Messerschmitt Bf 109, Boyd was not so lucky. He was chased out to sea by a German fighter as far as the French coast. Eventually the Messerschmitts broke off the pursuit and Boyd managed to get back to Westhampnett after two hours flying at the limit of his aircraft's endurance.

By August 1940, 145 Squadron had taken a battering. One particular day stands out as one of the worst – 8 August, 1940. The squadron was scrambled and ordered to intercept a formation of Ju 87 Stukas which, escorted by Bf 109s from *JG 27*, was attacking a convoy codenamed *Peewit*, which was heading west from Dover down the English Channel. With other squadrons from 11 Group, 145 Squadron engaged the enemy.

For his part, Squadron Leader Peel became embroiled in the melee which took place five miles south-east of St Catherine's Point on the Isle of Wight. In this action he claimed two Junkers Ju 87s destroyed, one damaged, one as unconfirmed, as well a Messerschmitt Bf 109E shot down. His squadron's score at the end of this ferocious dogfight was three Ju 87s shot down, six badly damaged and several escorting fighters also hit. As 145 Squadron headed back to Westhampnett to refuel and re-arm they left behind a badly mauled Convoy *Peewit*, four vessels of which had been sunk. After the morning's engagement Pilot Officer Lionel Sears and Sergeant Eric Baker failed to return; both men are still listed as 'Missing'.

Opposite: Personnel of 145 Squadron's 'B' Flight pictured at readiness outside one of Westhampnett's Nissen huts in July 1940. Seated on the far left is Flying Officer James Storrar, who was known as 'Jas', whilst immediately behind him, and almost hidden from view, is Pilot Officer Derek Forde. In the centre reading a book is Pilot Officer Archibald Weir. The individual on the far right is an Aircraftman runner. (The Andy Saunders Collection)

With almost no reprieve, the squadron was soon back in action just after 12.45 hours. Though it accounted for several more of the enemy, this was not without considerable loss. Pilot Officer Ernest Wakeham, Pilot Officer Lord Shuttleworth and Sub-Lieutenant Francis Smith RN (who was on loan to Fighter Command from the Fleet Air Arm) failed to return from the afternoon's operations.

Pilot Officer Peter Lawrence Parrott flew as a section leader on both sorties. In an interview in 1993 he recalled the following: "Well that was a convoy which was sailing along the south coast. We picked it up early in the morning with a section of three, just west of Beachy Head. There was one ship on fire; they had been attacked by E-boats during the night and we were sent out at dawn to check on them and also to give warning if there was a dawn raid by aircraft on them …

"There were three columns; they were small ships. One was burning and one was stopped in the water and there was a smallish naval ship – I think probably a destroyer, might have been a Corvette. It was a small destroyer laying a smoke screen and we flew over them for a little while and gave a bit of moral support I suppose. There was one little ship leading the land-side column flying a barrage balloon.

"We came back and landed and were scrambled at breakfast time. Climbing out over the coast due south, the convoy was now quite a lot further on, three hours at 15 knots or something. It was coming up to the Isle of Wight – it hadn't quite reached Selsey Bill.

"We had climbed due south and we were over it straight away and it was being attacked by Ju 87s. There was a mass of them and they were covered by 109s, and beyond them we could see another two waves of something like 80 to 100 aircraft, mixed Ju 87s and 109s.

"The first wave of Junkers were going down. The squadron commander put us into line astern – which was rather strange to me – but we went in line astern and then just picked our own target. I picked a Ju 87 which was just going down on its bombing run or at least had almost finished its

bombing run and I followed it up and started firing at it. He had started to turn to the south to go home but when I started firing he straightened up and then started going towards the land again. So I kept with him and gave him a short burst every now and again to make sure he knew I was there and he actually landed on the Isle of Wight, near Ventnor. He hit a tree at the end of his landing run and I had killed the rear gunner, but the pilot was ok; he was a prisoner of war.

"From the rest of the squadron, I think most people shot something down. We did two more sorties that day, one more in the afternoon … The squadron's commander, John Peel, was also shot down that day, he landed his aircraft on the Isle of Wight which turned over when it struck the ground and consequently he was in hospital. So it was five lost and one injured to the squadron … We were given a whole sheet of congratulatory telegrams from the AOC and the C-in-C and all the rest of it."[5]

Aircraftman Eric Marsden also recalled the squadron being given the day off and receiving a visit by Sir Archibald Sinclair, the then Secretary of State for Air: "Gradually we got things shaped up. And we now had beds. There were huge pits being excavated for air raid shelters. The pioneers were doing this work and had dug 8-9 feet deep holes, 20-30 feet long near our huts.

"On the first day of that battle [8 August was originally chosen as the start date for the Battle of Britain] 145 claimed twenty-one aircraft [shot]

Left: A small group of 145 Squadron personnel. Left to right are: Flying Officer Guy Rawstron Branch EGM, who was killed in action on 11 August 1940 whilst flying Hurricane P9251; Flight Lieutenant Adrian Hope Boyd, in the centre with the sunglasses; Flying Officer James Storrar, who racked up fifteen confirmed kills in the Battle of Britain; and Flight Lieutenant W. Pankratz, who was reported missing on 12 August. Not to be forgotten is Bill the dog. (Tangmere Military Aviation Museum)

Right: Flying Officer Guy Rawstron Branch EGM having a well-earned break between sorties outside 'B' Flight's hut with Bill the dog. After his death, Branch's Empire Gallantry Medal was exchanged for the newly-instituted George Cross. (Tangmere Military Aviation Museum)

down. We were given a day off and Archibald Sinclair came down and patted us all on the back. Boyd decided there should be a flight binge. So the pilots got in crates of beer and all of us were invited to the pilots' hut. We had a session, sitting round and I won't say ranks went by the board but there was a good deal of freedom and it was quite pleasant.

"One of our Corporals, a Welshman, had decided he needed to go out and look at the moon. No one noticed his absence for a while until we heard this wailing from the distance. He had fallen down this great pit dug for the air raid shelters. It was about 10-11pm at night; I had had two shandies and I was quite content to sit back and watch it. A few jumped in to help him out which meant that we were at the top watching with no intention to help. They were stuck down there overnight!"[6]

Such festivities aside, there was little respite for the men and machines of 145 Squadron. It was back in action on 11 August, engaging over 150 aircraft south of Swanage. Two more pilots were lost in this combat; even the commanding officer had to force-land again.

Pilot Officer Peter Parrot recalls the raid on the 11th: "We were getting a bit short of pilots by that time, five out of twenty [shot down] – we were down to fifteen pilots. On that day I had another go at a circle of 110s over Portsmouth. One I damaged I think because he put his nose down and started heading south – whether he got home I don't know.

"The 11th and 12th are mixed up in my mind. One of the raids was on Portsmouth, the other on Portland Bill, on the naval dockyard there. I am not sure if I went out to Portland; I certainly remember being over

Above: A 145 Squadron Hurricane makes a low pass over Westhampnett to show groundcrew that the guns have been fired, and to prepare fuel and ammunition ready for a quick turn round – which would be roughly eight minutes where possible. (Tangmere Military Aviation Museum)

Portsmouth and having a go there. Anyway we lost two more pilots on that day and on the following day we lost three more, so we had lost ten pilots, half the squadron, in five days, plus an 11th back on the 1st August."[7]

Still the battle waged on. On 12 August, 145 Squadron was airborne, pitching itself against large numbers of escorted Ju 88s just off the Isle of Wight, with the loss of three more valuable pilots.

By the time the squadron was moved from Westhampnett to Drem, in the heart of East Lothian, for a period of rest on 13 August, it had lost eleven pilots with another two wounded, nearly all between 8 and 12 of the

month. Indeed, when it flew out there were just three pilots left and the commanding officer.

With its period of rest and recuperation over, 145 Squadron soon moved south again, though this time to Tangmere, resuming sorties in October 1940.

The next unit in the firing line was 602 (City of Glasgow) Squadron, equipped with Spitfire Mk.Is. It had only been at RAF Westhampnett for four days when its pilots received their baptism of fire. Although the squadron only remained at Westhampnett for a short time, it experienced its fair share of the action.

The squadron was a pre-war Auxiliary Air Force unit formed in 1925 as a light bomber squadron. It had already proved itself on the outset of the war by shooting down the first German aircraft to fall on British soil, a Heinkel He 111 on 28 October 1939. The pilots had been in action from their base at Drem when the order was received by the CO, Squadron Leader A.V.R. 'Sandy' Johnstone, to move south to Westhampnett on 13 August 1940. They were to replace the severely depleted 145 Squadron.

On arrival at the West Sussex airfield, the 602 Squadron pilots were astonished to see a 145 Squadron Hurricane lying on its back in the middle of the field. Squadron Leader Peel, his arm in a sling after being injured, welcomed his relief and explained that his pilots, the ones who were left, were certainly ready for a rest.

Squadron Leader Sandy Johnston later recalled his reception: "Johnny Peel, the CO of 145 Squadron, was waiting to greet us, for it was his outfit we were here to relieve. He had an arm in a sling. According to Johnny, his outfit had been taking a bit of stick from Jerry and was now reduced to four aircraft and four pilots. That was his Hurricane in the middle of the airfield, he told me. He had brought it down without any aileron control. However, he was glad to say that the smoke rising from behind the hedge was coming from a burning Me 109! Westhampnett was beginning to sound more like Calamity Corner!"[8]

Writing a history of 602 Squadron in 1942 for its benevolent fund, the author F.G. Nancarrow also described the squadron's arrival at Westhampnett: "The Channel sky boiled with the puffs of bursting shells and the shapes of whirling planes when 602 Squadron flew into their new sector in the South area on the fateful 13th of August. 'There was one hell of a battle going on,' wrote one of the pilots. 'But as we were not fitted with the correct radio frequency we couldn't do anything about it.'"[9]

Squadron Leader Johnstone recorded his initial impressions of the airfield: "We have Westhampnett to ourselves, but it is nothing more than three large fields knocked into one with the old boundary fences replaced with camouflage paint … A belt of trees lines the eastern boundary, with two Nissen huts nestling underneath. These will do for the A Flight crew rooms. A further two Nissen huts on the north side will house B Flight, but they don't have any protection from trees.

"As for the living quarters, the airmen are billeted in buildings connected to dog kennels on the road to the racecourse, whilst the officers and NCOs have the use of empty farmhouses close to the airfield boundary. I am glad now that I insisted on having our camping equipment put on board the Harrows!"[10]

Nancarrow also described 602's new home: "The aerodrome to which they had been posted was little more than a large field, and billets were restricted to Nissen huts and tents. A farm-house nearby was taken over for messing purposes. It was something of an acquisition, being equipped

Right: Flight Lieutenant Boyd inspects German ammunition during a period of rest outside 'B' Flight's hut. Eric Marsden, one of the groundcrew who looked after Boyd's Hurricane, remembers that Boyd had a fixation with German ammunition and would often take it apart or, if he could not dismantle it, saw it in half. (The Andy Saunders Collection)

with a bath. In these surroundings, the Glasgow pilots and groundcrews settled down to what they imagined would amount only to a brief relief period of fighting."[11] As it turned out, there was to be little rest until a few days before Christmas.

Working as fast as they could, the men of 602 Squadron battled to bring their unit to readiness. It was at 06.50 hours the next day when they were called to action for the first time at Westhampnett. Following the scramble, a He 111 was located and attacked to the west of the airfield. The pilots undertook a further ten operational patrols that day.

It was pattern that remained little changed in the days that followed. "They were to be almost continuously 'at the ready' as a unit," continued Nancarrow. "For a good part of the time when invasion was thought to be imminent, the squadron not only maintained a constant watch in the air, but kept ceaseless vigil on the ground in case of a sudden attack by parachute troops on their aerodrome.

"For the first week the pilots and machines were put into the air from dawn till dusk and sometimes during the night by a skeleton maintenance crew. The mechanics, riggers, armourers, fitters worked like Trojans, hardly having time to sleep. They never let up for one minute until welcome relief came to them. Every man was a hero.

"During the hours of daylight they stood by the aircraft, sending them

Left: Flight Lieutenant Boyd manages to have a shave whilst at readiness outside the 'B' Flight hut. (Tangmere Military Aviation Museum)

Opposite: A rare, if poor quality, image of a Westhampnett-based squadron in action. In this case it is 'B' Flight of 145 Squadron taking off to the south-west sometime in early August 1940. The airfield's distinctive eastern boundary is visible in the background. (Tangmere Military Aviation Museum)

off in fighting trim, refuelling and rearmouring as they came back. Throughout the nights while the *Luftwaffe* thundered overhead and the blitz roared and echoed along the South Coast, they worked on the machines in the open air. There were no hangars, no benches, no permanent quarters. Fortunately, the weather was good. They lay beside the Spitfires to catch brief hours of sleep."[12] Such was life at Westhampnett in the early days.

Amongst the action during 602's early presence in Sussex was an engagement that occurred on 16 August. The squadron was ordered to scramble at midday, its instructions being to patrol over the airfield at 2,000 feet. The enemy had selected RAF Tangmere as its target and the Sector Station was already under attack when 'B' Flight's commander, Flight Lieutenant Robert Findlay Boyd, became airborne.

"Climbing at full throttle from the farm field [that was RAF Westhampnett] in the direction of Tangmere," wrote Nancarrow, "Boyd was just about to retract his undercarriage when he saw the angular shape of a Stuka streaking across his sights. It had dropped its load and was sweeping out of the target when it crossed Boyd's bow. Boyd pressed his gun-teat. His eight Brownings did the rest. The Nazi pilot probably never knew what hit him. He went straight on the ground, and Boyd, banking sharply, made a half circuit of the aerodrome and landed to rearm."

Despite his achievement, Boyd's subsequent combat report was as brief as the action it describes: "15 Ju 87s were seen diving in turn on Tangmere aerodrome and bombing, so 12 Spitfires took off at 13.00 hours to attack. I saw one Ju 87 pulling out of a dive and fired one short burst. Saw enemy aircraft crash through a hedge, returned and landed at 13:09."

Opposite: A group photograph of 602 (City of Glasgow) Squadron personnel taken outside the Officers' Mess at Westhampnett in 1940. The building forming the backdrop is Woodcote Farmhouse. Squadron Leader Sandy Johnstone is in the middle of the front row. The two squadron dogs are 'Crash', the Alsatian, and 'Belinda', which is being held by Pilot Officer Paddy Barthropp. 'Paddy' joined the squadron in mid-September 1940, which helps dates the picture. (The 602 (City of Glasgow) Squadron Museum)

Right: The south-facing elevation of Woodcote Farmhouse, the officers' accommodation for 602 Squadron. In fact, this house and the surrounding farm buildings were used for accommodation throughout the war, the former mainly for officers, the latter generally for groundcrew. This farmhouse features in many books and first-hand accounts. (The 602 (City of Glasgow) Squadron Museum)

"His combat report is probably unique in the history of Fighter Command," concluded Nancarrow. "For he was only in the air little more than half a minute from take-off to landing."

Later the same day, Findlay Boyd was airborne as part of Blue Section when it attacked a He 111 of *KG* 55 which had bombed the Great West aerodrome, now known as Heathrow Airport. "Successive attacks were delivered by section until the EA crashed in waste ground, approximate position North of Worthing," wrote Boyd, who was credited with the 'kill'.

Despite such frenetic activity, both in the air and on the ground, the squadron was often required to entertain official guests. This included His Royal Highness the Duke of Kent who visited Westhampnett on 22 August, staying for tea.

The airfield, meanwhile, was still suffering from a lack of even some basic facilities. This is alluded to by Sandy Johnstone who recalled in his memoir that because there were no permanent hangars the squadron had a canvas structure erected outside the field, requiring the Spitfires to still be taken through gaps in a hedge for maintenance. He also recalls airmen being billeted in the Goodwood Golf Club buildings and using the base of the race course grandstand for storing 602 Squadron's equipment.

The squadron suffered severely on 7 September 1940. This was the first day of the Blitz and most of the day's action took place over Kent as the German bombers headed for London. On this day the squadron's Operations Record Book (ORB) reveals that Air Chief Marshal Sir Cyril Newall, Chief of the Air Staff, visited the airfield. A month later, on 7 October, Air Vice Marshall Keith Park flew in to Westhampnett. He was followed, a week later, by Wing Commander the Duke of Hamilton who stayed with the squadron for the night.

As both the month of October, and indeed the Battle of Britain, drew to a close, Captain Cuthbert Orde arrived at Westhampnett to undertake portraits of some of the pilots – namely Flying Officer Micky Mount, Flight Lieutenant Robert Findlay Boyd, Flight Lieutenant Donald Jack and Sergeant Andrew McDowall.

By the time of Orde's visit, the weather had transformed the airfield into a sea of mud, especially in the vicinity of the dispersal huts, with the grass being torn up. The damp and cold conditions were to take their toll on the squadron's personnel – indeed, the ORB notes a shortage of pilots in November due to cold and influenza.

Up to this point, 602 Squadron had been flying Spitfires fitted with canvas-covered ailerons. This had led to considerable limitations regarding the combat effectiveness of the aircraft at high speeds. Jeffrey Quill, a Supermarine test pilot who had flown the Spitfire in combat, was aware of these issues and was committed to solving the problem.

On 19 December 1940, Quill arrived at Westhampnett. "I tested a pair of metal skinned ailerons with thin trailing edges on Spitfire R6718," he wrote. "The aeroplane was transformed … These ailerons were transferred to X4268 for check tests and on the 19th November I took this aircraft to Westhampnett where it was flown by the OC of 602 Squadron".[13]

After Sandy Johnstone had tested Quill's modification, it was clear that the new metal ailerons made a huge difference to the aircraft's high speed turning characteristics and word quickly spread throughout Fighter Command. Soon all the wing leaders and squadron commanders were trying to get their machines converted at Supermarine's Hamble aircraft works.

Above: 'A' Flight's Nissen hut at the dispersal, one of a small number of purpose built structures at Westhampnett used by both 145 and 602 squadrons. This one is on the eastern boundary of the airfield. (The 602 (City of Glasgow) Squadron Museum)

Opposite: The interior of one of the Nissen huts at Westhampnett – a picture which illustrates just how basic the accommodation on the airfield could be. Though a small stove has been provided to help keep the occupants warm, it is doubtful that the walls and windows would have done much to keep out the cold in the depths of winter. (The 602 (City of Glasgow) Squadron Museum)

Pilot Officer Nigel Rose had been with 602 Squadron from its first days at RAF Westhampnett and recalled both his arrival and his time whilst stationed there:

"The squadron left Drem, near Edinburgh on 13 August, 1940, we put

down at Church Fenton in Yorkshire for lunch and refuelling. A further hour and a half and we were circling Westhampnett, a satellite airfield to Tangmere, [which] was unpretentious, with no runways, hangars or other permanent buildings. There were a handful of Nissen huts and a small flint walled cottage in one corner.

"Catching the eye was the splendid spire of Chichester Cathedral about 2 miles in the west. Having taxied in, we began to get the feeling of our new surroundings. Our predecessors, 145 Squadron, flying Hurricanes, had lost 12 of their aircraft destroyed, with 11 pilots killed in the three days 8th, 11th and 12th August.

"On the 12th, the day previous to our arrival, 512 enemy planes had been plotted on Radar. 145 Squadron had, I recall, only 4 pilots left and they were forthwith despatched to Dyce [sic] in Scotland for recuperation. This was high drama, because although 602 had been bloodied earlier than most squadrons, during the defence of Scotland, the loss of a pilot and his aircraft was still a rarity. Things were now obviously on an altogether different scale.

"I wrote to my parents on the 14th August – 'we live for the moment in a typical Sussex Rectory with a delightful smell of soap, flowers and new mown grass. There are also wasps in abundance of which we bagged two 'certains' and three 'unconfirmed' at tea just after we arrived …

"After only a day or two, we ourselves began to see casualties in both pilots and aircraft. MacLean and Urie were seriously wounded and after a particularly violent engagement it was not unusual to see one or more of our Spitfires limping back with crippling damage. Some could be repaired on site or at Tangmere, but often they would be transported to a maintenance unit for reconstruction, or writing off!

"The fine summer of 1940 made for days that seemed so long. The morning call to 'flights' could be as early as 4 a.m and sometimes a scramble would mean taking off in a blanket of mist, above which the only point of reference was the spire of the Cathedral bathed pink in the rising sun.

"Release at dusk on a fine day could be as late as 9pm. In an average day, a pilot would fly 3 or 4 sorties. Sometimes the plot which had caused the scramble would turn out to be bogus and we would return without incident. Engaged or not, the groundcrews of fitters, riggers and armourers would be swarming over the Spitfires, and the refuelling bowser would be instantly in action. The whole turnaround was overseen with incredible efficiency by the Flight Sergeant.

"In 1940 the squadron was still flying in four sections of three. 'A' Flight, comprising red and yellow sections, and 'B' flight, blue and green. This formation was later abandoned as too clumsy and a switch made to six pairs of leader and 'tail guard' – a much more manoeuvrable arrangement learned, I believe, from the *Luftwaffe*.

"An average sortie from Westhampnett would be like this: The phone in the flight hut would ring with the message 'Villa Squadron, Scramble Mayfield, Angels 20'. A race over to the cockpits then took place with ground crews already in position starting engines, helping to do up parachute straps and harnesses – and chocks away.

"The Sector Controller at Tangmere was being fed the latest information from Group Headquarters, where Radar and Observer Corps plots were collected, so numbers, heights and direction of raids were continuously monitored. The Sector Controller could then advise the Squadron Leader.

"As we were climbing to 20,000 feet above the centre of Sussex the

Right: A group of 602 Squadron pilots, all from 'B' Flight, pictured outside one of the dispersal huts at Westhampnett. Second from right is Flight Lieutenant Donald MacFarlane Jack who claimed a Junkers Ju 88 as damaged in July and a Bf 110 and a Bf 109 destroyed in August 1940. Jack went on to command 123 Squadron and then 80 Squadron in the Middle East, ending the war as a Wing Commander. (The 602 (City of Glasgow) Squadron Museum)

Controller could adjust the vector and rate of climb, where possible, and, if time, to give us the advantage of both height and sun.

"An average mass attack would comprise fifty bombers, either Heinkels, Dorniers or Ju 88s. Accompanied by fifty or so fighters … For a green pilot, just joined the squadron without the benefit of an Operational Training Unit (as happened to some of us immediately following the evacuation of Dunkirk), it was an awesome sight to see the serried ranks of hostile aircraft, made all the clearer at times by being silhouetted against a blanket of white cloud.

"The Commanding Officer would divide the squadron so that one flight was allocated to the fighters, one to the bombers. If the bombers were slower and easier targets, they still had the protection of their turret gunners. More often than not in 602 we seemed to find ourselves tangling with the fighter escort.

"Having selected your target, you would turn your gun button on the control column to 'fire' and the next most important action was to ensure, as best you could, that you were not being targeted yourself! Your own attack would usually be made from a stern or quarter beam. The former

Opposite: Some of 602 Squadron's groundcrew pose in front of Spitfire 'LO-H', this being the aircraft flown by Charles Hector MacLean. MacLean claimed a Junkers Ju 87 damaged on 18 August 1940. Eight days after that he engaged a formation of He 111 bombers but was subsequently hit by cannon fire from a Bf 109 which all but severed his foot. He 'belly-landed' at Tangmere and as he was lifted from the cockpit his foot remained in the aircraft. His leg was subsequently amputated below the knee. Unable to continue flying, MacLean became a fighter controller, remaining in the RAF until the 1950s. This photograph was taken in front of Fishers Cottage, the NCO pilots' quarters located on the airfield's eastern boundary. (The 602 (City of Glasgow) Squadron Museum)

was the most deadly, and anyone who has studied camera gun films will confirm this.

"A beam attack meant allowing correct 'Deflection' – i.e. the aim through the gun sight must be drawn forward to lead the target before firing. Some pilots such as Archie McKellar were known to favour a head on attack. This was difficult to achieve but hugely demoralising to the opposing bombers.

"You often hear the term 'dogfight', but in World War II the actual engagement was usually very brief. The instant reaction if you were being attacked was to go in to the steepest turn you could manage to try and get on the attacker's tail. This would usually mean losing consciousness temporarily. Or you could turn on your back and dive right out, twisting and turning this way and that. Such a manoeuvre doesn't sound very brave, but sometimes to run away allowed one to live and fight another day!

"On levelling out from a 400 mph dive it was quite astonishing how empty the sky was and often not a plane to be seen. Occasionally in the middle of a chaotic scrap, a Bf 109 or 110 would flash past you going in the opposite direction with breathtaking closing speed. There was little time to do anything but gawp and say a little prayer.

"Of course not every day was suitable for flying, but after a busy period there was a need for relaxation. In the evening you could drink in the mess or at the local pubs, but with early starts, heavy partying was not really an option.[14] The Squash Club in Chichester made us honorary members and this provided a much appreciated diversion. Here I met Pamela, whom I was to marry the following year.

"After the end of September, the mass raids over West Sussex began to drop off and we were more often than not vectored on to incidents over East Sussex and Kent, but we were still flying an average of three to four sorties a day when the weather allowed.

"Being an RAF fighter pilot (top button of your tunic undone) gave one

a definite feel of pride and perhaps importance. Yet there was certainly no recognition that the outcome of our activities would be such a crucial contribution to the progress of the war as it ultimately turned out.

"Mind you not everybody loved us. We had a number of reasons for suspecting sabotage to our Spitfires. One such rather dramatic example of this was Spitfire L1019, a relatively old plane which had, from an encounter, been badly damaged. It was despatched to a Maintenance Unit and some months later the Commanding Officer was informed by CID that upon stripping the engine, two small packets of dynamite had been found wired to the exhaust manifold! All of us had flown this aircraft several times. This example of misanthropy is puzzling, but one has to remember that in 1940, Communists were sympathetic to the Germans, an attitude that vanished when Hitler invaded Russia in 1941!

"By Christmas the powers that be decided that 602 Squadron should be transferred to the north for a rest."[15]

For 602 Squadron, its efforts whilst stationed at Westhampnett were recognised by the award of three Distinguished Flying Crosses and three Distinguished Flying Medals. The cost, though, was high, with six of its pilots having been lost on operations.

On 17 December 1940, 602 Squadron departed for Prestwick and a much-needed break.

Left: Sergeant George Whipps in the cockpit of a 602 Squadron Spitfire at Westhampnett. Whipps joined the squadron at Drem on 21 June 1940. He was shot down following combat with Bf 109s over Hailsham, East Sussex, on 6 September 1940, but baled out unhurt. Interestingly, his aircraft, N3227, finally fell to earth at Peasmarsh – some twenty-five miles away. (The Andy Saunders Collection)

Left: A Spitfire of 602 Squadron ready at dispersal, plugged into the 'trolley acc', or accumulator, ready for a scramble. This image was taken on the eastern boundary of the airfield. (The 602 (City of Glasgow) Squadron Museum)

Below Left: Squadron Leader Sandy Johnstone comes into land across Westhampnett's eastern boundary in Spitfire X4162. Coded 'LO-J', this was Johnstone's regular mount. This aircraft suffered a flying accident in November 1940, but was repaired and transferred to 124 Squadron.

Below: A snapshot of 602 Squadron pilots at rest outside one of the flight huts at Westhampnett. (The 602 (City of Glasgow) Squadron Museum)

Left: Sergeant Mervyn Herbert Sprague of 602 Squadron on his wedding day. He was shot down on 25 August 1940, but managed to bale out. Later, on 11 September 1940, he was shot down and killed following combat with Bf 110s south of Selsey Bill, whilst flying Spitfire N3282. His body was washed ashore on 10 October. Until the moment the Channel gave him up, his wife visited the airfield every day awaiting his return. He is buried in Tangmere Churchyard. (The Andy Saunders Collection)

Right: Pilot Officer Osgood Villiers 'Pedro' Hanbury poses in front of his Spitfire at Westhampnett. Having joined 602 Squadron on 3 September 1940, Hanbury soon made his mark, claiming two Dornier Do 17s on 7 and 12 September respectively, and a Bf 110 destroyed on 15 September. A shared Ju 88 was recorded on the 30th, a damaged Ju 88 on 5 October and finally a Bf 109 destroyed on 30 October. He did not survive the war; the aircraft he was travelling to Gibraltar in was shot down over the Bay of Biscay in 1943. (The Andy Saunders Collection)

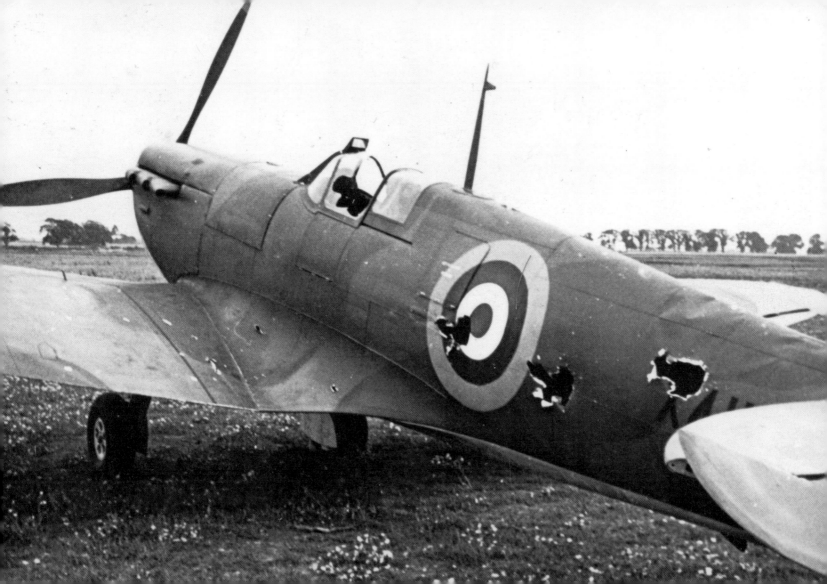

Left: Flight Lieutenant John Dunlop Urie flew 602 Squadron's Spitfire X4110 on 18 August 1940, whilst engaging a force of Ju 87s and Bf 109s over nearby Ford. As can be seen here, Urie's aircraft was hit by cannon shells from a Bf 109, causing damage to his fuselage, his flaps, and puncturing a tyre. His legs were also hit by metal splinters but he managed to achieve a safe landing back at Westhampnett. Urie survived the war having attained the rank of wing commander. (The Andy Saunders Collection)

Above: Two further views of X4110 and the damaged caused by a Bf 109 on 18 August 1940. This aircraft was struck off charge on 5 October 1940. (Alfred Price via Peter Arnold)

Opposite page: Spitfires Mk.Is of 'A' Flight, 602 Squadron parked near the northern boundary of the airfield. The Spitfires with visible codes are 'LO-B', 'LO-X' and, in the background, 'LO-G'. 'LO-G' was X4382, which was flown by Pilot Officer 'Pedro' Hanbury, who claimed two confirmed kills, and one damaged, in this aircraft. (The 602 (City of Glasgow) Squadron Museum)

Above: Spitfire Mk.I X4382, coded 'LO-G', which was flown by Pilot Officer 'Pedro' Hanbury, pictured on Westhampnett's eastern boundary with tented accommodation for some of the groundcrew visible in the background. This aircraft was handed over to 610 (County of Chester) Squadron on 14 December 1940, and remained at Westhampnett until March of 1941. (The Andy Saunders Collection)

Opposite page: Pilot Officer Nigel Rose pictured on his Spitfire at dispersal on the eastern boundary of the airfield. Rose claimed a Bf 110 on 25 August and another shared on 7 September. He was injured on 11 September but returned to flying on 7 October to see out the end of the Battle of Britain. He remained with 602 Squadron until 2 September 1941, when he was posted to 54 Squadron. Rose survived the war and became a chartered surveyor. (The Andy Saunders Collection)

Right: Pilot Officer Archibald Lyall in his Mae West at Westhampnett. He was with 602 Squadron when it first arrived there. During his time at the West Sussex airfield, he achieved a number of kills, his tally eventually amounting to three destroyed, three shared, two probable, five damaged and four shared damaged. He was shot down over the Isle of Wight on 28 November 1940, but baled out too low from Spitfire N3242. He died aged 27 and was cremated at Woodvale Crematorium, Brighton. (The Andy Saunders Collection)

Above and Opposite: A series of photos showing the rescue of 602 Squadron's Sergeant Pilot Cyril Babbage at Bognor Regis on 26 August 1940. Babbage had engaged a Bf 109, shooting it down, only to then be attacked by *Hauptmann* Mayer of 1/*JG* 53. His Spitfire, X4118, was severely damaged and he took to his parachute. Babbage was awarded a Distinguished Flying Medal on 25 October 1940. (The Andy Saunders Collection)

Opposite and this page: The aftermath of another incident involving Sergeant Pilot Cyril Babbage. He was engaged in combat with a Junkers Ju 88 over the Channel on 12 October 1940, when return fire damaged his aircraft, Spitfire X4541. Babbage made a force-landing at Iford Farm near Lewes in East Sussex, during which his aircraft overturned. Whilst Babbage was miraculously unhurt, the Spitfire was struck off charge after only six-and-a-half hours of flying time. (The Andy Saunders Collection)

Opposite page: A Junkers Ju 88 of *LG* 1 that was shot down at Mudberry Farm, Bosham, by Westhampnett-based Spitfires of 602 Squadron on 21 September 1940. Note the shield of a red griffon on a white background of *LG* 1. (Historic Military Press)

Above: Some of 602 Squadron's groundcrew pictured outside a dispersal at Westhampnett in 1940. (The 602 (City of Glasgow) Squadron Museum)

Right: Another victim of Westhampnett-based fighters, in this case the Heinkel He 111P of 7./*Kampfgeschwader* 55, which fell to the guns of Flight Lieutenant Robert Findlay Boyd on 16 August 1940. Coded G1+FR, it crashed at High Salvington, north of the West Sussex coastal resort of Worthing. (The Andy Saunders Collection)

Opposite page: The Heinkel 111P, shot down by Sergeant Basil Whall of 602 Squadron on 26 August, crashed on the beach at East Wittering. Coded G1+DM, this 4/*KG*55 aircraft was riddled with some 500 bullet holes. (The Andy Saunders Collection)

Right: Sergeant Basil Ewart Patrick Whall of 602 Squadron, who claimed the He 111P at East Wittering. Whall's subsequent combat report relating to the events of 26 August 1940, states: "I was Green 3 and took off from W. Hampnett 16.13 hrs. After attacking 2 Me 109s without any visible damage to them I dived down onto bombers, selecting one He 111 on flank of mass of bombers on S.E. course. Adopted full beam. Attacked slightly in front from 1000 feet above and saw port engine stop and E/A drop out of formation. Followed this E/A/ down doing 4 more attacks all on the beam and saw second engine stop and port engine flame. This E/A landed on beach at W. Wittering. Circled till I saw Army taking crew prisoner then climbed to attack single He 111 flying S below cloud at 1000 ft. Caught this E/A 10 miles out to sea and adopted Quarter attack starboard side from above. Starborard engine belching clouds of white smoke and E/A caught fire and crashed in sea. I then returned to land at W. Hampnett, pausing to circle round pilot of friendly fighter in water." (The Andy Saunders Collection)

One of 602 Squadron's pilots, Sergeant Douglas Elcome, pictured in his aircraft, nicknamed *Goofy*, at RAF Westhampnett. Elcome had joined the squadron at Drem on 21 June 1940. Whilst flying from Westhampnett, Elcome destroyed a Bf 109 over Dungeness on 31 August, before subsequently landing, following this combat, with a damaged glycol tank at Ford. He failed to return from a routine patrol on 26 October 1940. (The Andy Saunders Collection)

As 1940 drew to a close the *Luftwaffe*'s offensive had slackened during daylight with much of its effort being concentrated during the hours of darkness. As the squadrons of Fighter Command were no longer constantly in action, there was an opportunity to re-arm and prepare for the next phase of the air war. It was time to go on the offensive.

The objective of this new stance – 'Reaching Out' as it came to be known – was to encourage enemy fighters into the air over Continental Europe so that they could be engaged by the RAF. Fighter Command's pilots were also to attack 'targets of opportunity' on the ground as well as escorting bombing raids on selected targets. These operations were to be known by a strange mix of codewords such as *Circuses, Ramrods, Rangers, Roadsteads* and *Rhubarbs*.

It was as early as 10 January 1941 that the RAF conducted its first *Circus* mission. This was the codename given to operations where bombers with a heavy fighter escort were sent over the Channel with the intention of drawing enemy fighters into combat. A *Ramrod* was similar to a *Circus*, but with the intention of destroying a target. A *Ranger*, meanwhile, was a large formation intrusion over enemy territory with the aim of wearing down the enemy fighter force; a *Roadstead* was a low-level attack on coastal shipping; and a *Rhubarb* was small-scale freelance fighter sortie against ground targets of opportunity.

The despatch on air operations, written by Marshal of the Royal Air Force Sir Sholto Douglas, provides an insight into the intent and strategic aims of the RAF at that time:

"During the Battle of Britain the initiative in daylight operations lay with the Germans. Nevertheless, even before the battle was over a time

Above: Some of 302 Squadron's personnel at Westhampnett. Left to right are: Sergeant Marian Rytka, who claimed a total of three destroyed and one probable before being killed in a Spitfire crash in December 1942; Pilot Officer Marceli Neyder, who claimed a Ju 88 damaged over Selsey Bill on 13 March 1941 and went on to claim a further three aircraft destroyed and two damaged before being killed in action whilst flying a de Havilland Mosquito with 23 Squadron; Pilot Officer Władysław Gnyś; Flying Officer Marian Duryasz, who ended the war as a squadron leader; and Sergeant Antoni Beda, who flew with the squadron during the Battle of Britain before serving with Nos. 87, 301, 304 and 307 squadrons. Beda survived the war and moved to the USA. (Via P. Sikora)

Previous page: Sergeant Marian Domagala of 302 (Polish) Squadron, who was posted in during its last month at RAF Westhampnett, sat in his Hurricane on the airfield's characteristic grass runways. (Andy Saunders)

Right: Pilot Officer Edward Roman Pilch joined 302 Squadron during the Battle of Britain, during which he claimed a Do 17 and a Ju 88. Whilst flying from Westhampnett he claimed a share in the destruction of a Ju 88 on 16 February 1941. He was killed during a practice dogfight over Arundel on 20 February 1941. His Hurricane, R2687 'WX-X', was last seen diving towards the ground from 15,000 feet emitting smoke and flames. He is buried in Chichester Cemetery. (Via P. Sikora)

was foreseen when our fighter squadrons would seize the initiative and engage the German fighters over the far side of the Channel. The necessary operational instructions were drawn up as early as the third week in October, 1940, and revised in the first week of December.

"By the latter date it was possible to contemplate something more ambitious than a mere pushing forward of fighter patrols, and on 29th November, I instructed the Air Officer Commanding No.II Group to look into the possibility of combining offensive sweeps with operations by Bomber Command.

"In the middle of December the German fighter force, which had suffered heavy losses since the summer, virtually abandoned the offensive for the time being. Clearly, the moment had come to put our plans into effect and wrest the initiative from the enemy. Broadly speaking, the plan which we now adopted visualised two kinds of offensive operations. In cloudy weather, small numbers of fighters would cross the channel under cover of the clouds, dart out of them to attack any German aircraft they could find, and return similarly protected. In good weather fighter forces amounting to several squadrons at a time, and sometimes accompanied by bombers, would sweep over Northern France. The codenames chosen for these operations were respectively 'Mosquito' (later changed to 'Rhubarb', to avoid confusion with the aircraft of that name) and 'Circus'; but in practice it was necessary to restrict the name 'Circus' to operations with bombers, and fulfilling certain other conditions which will become apparent as this account proceeds.

"'Rhubarb' patrols were begun on 20th December, 1940, and provided valuable experience alike for pilots, operational commanders, and the staffs of the formations concerned. I encouraged the delegation of responsibility for the planning of these patrols to lower formations, and many patrols were planned by the pilots themselves with the help of their Squadron Intelligence Officers."[1]

Unsurprisingly, the Westhampnett-based pilots and aircraft found themselves in the thick of the action, albeit after a slow start. As the year progressed the home squadrons were flying daily sorties as part of the Tangmere Wing, including some of the early offensive operations.

On 23 November 1940, the airfield became home to 302 (Polish) Squadron which moved in from RAF Northolt under the command of Squadron Leader Mieczyslaw Mümler. The squadron had formed at Leconfield in July 1940 and was initially equipped with Hurricane Mk.Is. It was involved in the final stages of the Battle of Britain.

During the early part of December, 302 Squadron acclimatised to its new home, undertaking local familiarisation flights and engine tests. However, the weather was again to play its part with Westhampnett declared non-operational for a number of days during the month and into January 1941. This resulted in plans to install a full perimeter track with dispersal areas. At the same time, the airmen's accommodation was upgraded and hangars installed.

On 19 December 1940, 610 (County of Chester) Squadron moved in, sharing Westhampnett with the Poles, though the latter seem to have been mostly used for standing patrols.

Both units were visited by Air Vice-Marshal Trafford Leigh Mallory on 8 January 1941 after he had inspected RAF Tangmere. With the New Year both squadrons continued to take part in operations, including *Circus* 3 on

5 February, when they provided target support to bombers attacking an airfield at St Omer. Their ORBs show that they carried out practice scrambles and attacks, including formation flying, through into February 1941. It was one of these exercises that ended in disaster for Sergeant Antoni Markiewicz who, flying Hurricane V6753, struck the sea whilst diving on a target marker. He was able reach the shore where he crash-landed. Markiewicz was taken to the Royal West Sussex Hospital in Chichester suffering from minor injuries.

This was not the only flying accident to affect 302 Squadron during this period. On 14 February 1941, one of 610 Squadron's Spitfires landed on top of a 302 Squadron Hurricane dispersed on the airfield, killing a Polish rigger, Aircraftman Jan Przybyłowski, who was sitting in the cockpit, and injuring the fitter standing on the wingtip. Przybyłowski was buried in Chichester Cemetery.

Bad luck persisted for the squadron when, on 20 February, Pilot Officer Edward Pilch was killed in a flying accident after taking part in a practice dogfight over Arundel. His aircraft dived in to the ground from 15,000 feet emitting smoke and flame.

On 13 March 1941, 'A' Flight, consisting of Pilot Officer Wacław Król,

---

Right: With one of 302 Squadron's Westhampnett-based Hurricanes as a backdrop, the pilots in this image are, from left to right, as follows: Pilot Officer Marceli Neyder; Pilot Officer Władysław Gnyś; Sergeant Marian Rytka; Sergeant Antoni Beda; and Flying Officer Stanislaw Chalupa. Chalupa opened his score against the enemy whilst serving in the Polish Air Force when he claimed one shared victory. He then joined the *Armée de l'Air*, adding to his tally whilst flying the Morane 406. He escaped to Britain at the fall of France and joined 302 Squadron in late July 1940. He finished the war with a score of three destroyed, four shared destroyed, two probable and two shared probables and one damaged. (Via P. Sikora)

Pilot Officer Marceli Neyder and Pilot Officer B. Bernas, engaged a Junkers Ju 88 at 27,000 feet over Selsey Bill. The subsequent combat report, filled out by Król, states:

"I took off with another two aircraft at 16:10 hours as leader of Blue Section to patrol St Catherine's Point. After patrolling for 20 minutes I received an order to fly in the direction of Selsey Bill at 30,000 ft. Whilst climbing on this course I was given a vector of 180° and I was informed that an e/a [enemy aircraft] was approaching the English Coast from the South, five miles away. Whilst flying in this course I saw the enemy aircraft at 27,000 ft, which I identified as a Ju 88. I climbed making a turn up sun. The enemy did not see us at first, not until we had approached to within 500 yards, did a turn of 180° down sun and began to dive from 27,000 ft to just above sea level. Whilst turning we attacked the e/a sometimes with another aircraft from the quarter above and up sun."[2]

The German rear gunner was observed to keep returning fire until the Ju 88 reached sea level, at which point the Polish pilots ceased their attack due to lack of ammunition and fuel. They landed back at Westhampnett at 17.10 hours claiming one aircraft damaged.

The pilots and groundcrew of 302 Squadron departed for Kenley on 6 April. For its part, 610 Squadron remained in residence at Westhampnett longer than the Poles and operated alongside 616 (South Yorkshire) Squadron as part of the Tangmere Wing. An Auxiliary Air Force squadron, 610 was based at Acklington, Northumberland, when, on 14 December 1940, it received orders to move south, arriving at Westhampnett on 19 December 1940.

It remained at the Sussex airfield throughout the summer of 1941. At this time it was commanded by Acting Squadron Leader John Ellis who had joined 610 at RAF Wittering at the outbreak of the war and fought over Dunkirk and through the Battle of Britain. Ellis remained the squadron's CO until May 1941 when he was replaced by Squadron Leader Ken Holden.

As the men of 610 Squadron settled in at Westhampnett, Fishers Cottage, the thatched building inside the airfield boundary, was used as sergeants' accommodation, whilst the cottages up by the threshold to the present day Runway 24 served as both billets and cookhouse.

The officers continued to be accommodated across the road in the main farmhouse at Woodcote Farm. At this stage of the war several new corrugated iron hangars were being erected on the airfield for maintenance. It is also stated in some accounts that such work was undertaken in a number of barns to the east of the airfield, just to the south of Westerton, though these have long since been demolished.

An insight in to life at Westhampnett during this period of the war is provided by one off 610 Squadron's groundcrew, or 'erks' as they were commonly referred to – although his name is not known. It is interesting to note that elsewhere in his account, the writer mentions the postal address for the airfield was actually RAF Woodcote. Having confirmed that the officers were billeted at Woodcote Farm, he adds the following:

"The Sergeants' Mess was in a pair of thatched cottages nearby. The 'erbets' – well they slept anywhere. Most of them slept under the Grandstand on the racecourse, others in the 'Totaliser' Room on the racecourse, some in a couple of tents on the airfield. However, me, Jack

Right: This trio of 302 Squadron pilots are, again left to right, Pilot Officer Marceli Neyder, Pilot Officer Wacław Król, and Pilot Officer Bronislaw Bernas. Król subsequently went on to be an Ace with a recorded score of nine destroyed, three probables and four damaged. Ending the war with the rank of wing commander, he received numerous Polish awards for valour as well as the Distinguished Flying Cross. Bernas was also a pre-war Polish pilot who was called up on 24 August 1939. He fought in Poland and escaped via France to Britain, being posted to 302 Squadron on 23 September 1940. (Via P. Sikora)

Kendrick, and Wallie Howard, we slept in the next field to the landing ground. In this field was an ancient agricultural building, which had been converted into an aircraft hangar for a light aircraft which was owned, and before the war, flown by the Duke.

"It was divided by a 'chicken wire' partition. The immobilized aircraft was in one part and we chaps had our beds in the other. Later we were moved up to the Totaliser building.

"There were absolutely no facilities at all [at Westhampnett]. At the barn we had a small two-wheeled water bowser, and some tin bowls in which to both bath and wash. Washing was done outside while hiding behind a hedge, which partly screened us from the road.

"There wasn't a NAAFI or such refinement in the true sense. However, the Naafi had done its best. They erected a small marquee, signed up a couple of old men of pensionable age, and they boiled water in an outside boiler, made tea, sold the cakes, then, about four-thirty, they 'cashed-up', washed up, and took the cash over to Tangmere.

"Our 'Kitchen' for the 'Cookhouse' was a large circle of brickwork about five feet high, with a gap in the brickwork for an 'entrance'. It was in fact the farm's dung heap or 'midden'. We cleaned out all the cow dung and stinking straw, put in some trestle tables and soup cauldrons etc, and it was 'the kitchen'. Later, the 'Works and Bricks' Department at Tangmere worked wonders and found some corrugated iron sheets to fashion a roof.

"Finally we had luxury indeed – they sent in a 'trailer kitchen'. This was a caravan cookhouse as supplied to the featherbedded Army. That brought extra work for the engine fitters, as one was supplied every day as 'duty fitter' on the kitchen equipment – cleaning the paraffin burners etc.

"All food when cooked was carried about ten yards to an open-fronted cart shed, in which had neatly been placed some trestle tables. However, God help you when it rained because the rain lashed in, soaked you, and filled the plates with rainwater. This was cured when some agency managed to find a roll of thick green canvas, similar to that used as a 'tilt'

on a lorry. This was fixed to the roof beam below the gutter, left rolled up in fine weather, and rolled down when it rained.

"Meanwhile there was trouble with the Army regiment which had been sent in to guard the airfield – they threatened mutiny because they alleged that they just could not eat the food the Air Force was living on. Hard luck you Pongos!!"[3]

December 1940 was a relatively quiet period, with 610 Squadron carrying out standing patrols. There was a little excitement on Christmas Day when two pilots, Flight Lieutenant Constantine Pegge and Flight Lieutenant Nigel Drever, encountered a Ju 88 over Westhampnett – it was above the cloud and both Spitfires were unable to get within firing range.

On 10 January 1941, the squadron participated in one of the first offensive sweeps across the Channel. Heading to the area between Calais and Dunkirk at 25,000 feet, no enemy aircraft were encountered and all of 610's aircraft returned safely to Westhampnett.

These first operations across the Channel, as well as Westhampnett in general, were described by Sergeant Herbert David Denchfield:

"When we reached Westhampnett, Blue Section pulled up to about 5000ft to cover Red and Yellow, as each swung into echelon starboard to approach and land using an anti-clockwise approach. Nearby, Tangmere (our sector station) flew clockwise circuits. Having parked the aircraft about 50 yds apart in a haphazard saw-tooth pattern to limit damage from ground-strafing aircraft, we wandered over for lunch and were then released until 9 a.m. the following morning.

"There was a subtly different atmosphere now, possibly because we

---

Right: During their time at Westhampnett, 302 Squadron was visited in March 1941 by the Duke of Kent, who is seen here talking to Marian Wedzik. It is not known where the hut in the background was located on the airfield. (Via P. Sikora)

were now a close-knit fighting squadron with no more regular basic training to do. In fact we seldom flew singly, or for instruction, from now on. Significantly, whereas at Acklington we'd had a history of continuing accidents, mostly of the avoidable kind, I cannot recall one accident at Westhampnett. Basically we each now had one particular aircraft to fly, although we did sometimes fly others, and this gave each of us a particular rigger and fitter to look after and sometimes to allow us to use their aircraft …

"The airfield lay about 2 miles north-west of Tangmere and was all grass at that time. Nowadays the Goodwood motor racetrack runs round what was later the perimeter track. The road to Chichester ran along the eastern side to join a small country lane along the north side at a crossroads in the north-east corner.

"In this corner sat a farmhouse [Woodcote] and outbuildings in which some of the non-flying activities took place – the aircrew NCOs had one room as a dining room – along with the Poles from the Hurricane squadron, 302, that shared the airfield. 'A' Flight was dispersed just along the west side from the crossroads, and 'B' Flight was along the small country road, running back from the crossroads.

"Each flight had a Nissen hut containing a couple of beds, chairs, telephone and all the other clobber necessary in a flight office and pilot's crew room. A clockwork gramophone on which were played incessantly our favourites; 'Mr Paganini', 'She had to go and lose it at the Astor', 'The Bulbul Emir' etc. The gramophone was an essential part of the time we spent at readiness, and gave a background to our innumerable games of 'clobber' (ludo to you!) whilst sitting at readiness. Each flight had an Elsan [toilet] in an outside hut.

"The officers were quartered in a large house – I can't recall if this was Woodcote near the crossroads, or Goodwood House itself. The aircrew NCOs were in a largish cottage in its own grounds just behind 'B' Flight [Fishers Cottage]. Billy Raine and myself were in a large downstairs room,

Right: Photographed beside his personal aircraft, Hurricane Mk.II Z2773 (coded 'WX-T'), Pilot Officer Tadeusz Czerwinski was one of the most successful Polish airmen during the Battle of France. He served as 302 Squadron's 'B' Flight commander from December 1940. He claimed four enemy aircraft destroyed during his time in France, with 302 Squadron in the Battle of Britain and in early 1942 whilst serving with 306 Squadron flying Spitfires. Czerwinski was shot down and killed whilst undertaking a *Rhubarb* in the St Omer area on 22 August 1942. At the time he was 306 Squadron's CO. (Via P. Sikora)

later joined by Sam Hamer. A sitting room led off this, as did the stairs to the upstairs rooms used by Hamlyn, Bill Ballard and the other NCO pilots. Two erks had a small room off ours alongside a kitchen, and they kept the place clean, woke us up for early morning readiness and generally looked after us with great dedication. There was also a garage. The airmen were quartered in all sorts of barns and buildings, and I believe some were actually up at the Goodwood horse racing track itself, but I can't recall where the ground staff senior NCOs were living.

"There were no hangars and all routine maintenance was carried out in the open. All this in freezing conditions, and then to live and sleep in a barn! I think our groundcrew suffered greatly in ensuring our aircraft were in tip-top condition, and yet, if my own rigger and fitter were typical (as I know they were), they were never less than cheerful and co-operative. For more complicated maintenance the aircraft were hauled across the road behind 'B' Flight through gaps in the hedges and up a rough track to a large barn."

Of 610 Squadron's duties whilst stationed at Westhampnett, Denchfield recalled the following: "As well as day patrols, we also had to fly as night interceptors. Spits were not designed for this! Every night each of the squadrons in the Tangmere Wing, we and 302 at Westhampnett, and 65 at

Tangmere, allocated three pilots to the scheme. Each pilot had a specific height at which to fly and a code number.

"When in operation the aircraft were staggered up at 1,000ft intervals from a pre-arranged datum height with 'Layer 1' at the lowest level and 'Layer 9' at the highest. When scrambled the datum height and zero hour were known, and the pilots had to be at height just outside the patrol area by zero hour. Until then the 'ack-ack' [anti-aircraft guns] would be heaving all sorts of muck and corruption over the patrol area so it was wise to keep out 'til zero. All ack-ack was to cease at zero whereupon the nine hopefuls would surge in to patrol, each at his designated height, looking for trouble.

"Our order was 'aircraft with more than one engine are to be attacked'. This came in the course of a meeting of all the pilots in the Wing, held in the Officer's Mess at Tangmere. One lad asked what if one was sure the suspect aircraft was, in fact, British, and was told that as no self-respecting bomber crew would fly into what was clearly a defended area under attack, one could assume the aircraft was a phony, and the order stood … Our normal patrol area was one of a ten mile radius from the centre of Southampton or Portsmouth, as the case might be.

"Most mornings I was awakened at about 6am, while it was still pitch black, hearing, half awake, the first uncertain coughing of a Merlin followed by the sudden rasping roar as she caught, reducing to a subdued rumble as the erk throttled back to let her warm, and sat waiting for the temperatures to stabilise before starting his checks. This sole engine would be followed by others in quick succession until a steady throb of maybe 12 or 14 Merlins intruded into that delightful hiatus twixt waking and sleeping.

"Then Taffy would bring the tea, and say 'readiness in 5 minutes'. Then followed five delicious minutes sitting drinking tea exchanging the odd monosyllabic comment with Billy or Sam if they were also on readiness, and then the shocking plunge out into the freezing atmosphere beyond the blankets. A quick wash and shave, dress in the 'working blue'; throw

Right: Sergeant Eugeniusz Jan Adam Nowakiewicz fought in Poland with 123 Fighter Squadron, managing to escape by flying his aircraft to Romania. From there he was able to reach France, where, flying in the *Armée de l'Air*, he shared in the destruction of a He 111. Nowakiewicz arrived in the United Kingdom in July 1940 and, like many of his compatriots, joined 302 Squadron in August that year. He claimed a probable Ju 88 in October, before being wounded in combat with Bf 109s on 8 November, making a force-landing at Detling. Another Bf 109 was added to his score in May 1941. He was subsequently shot down by anti-aircraft fire near Boulogne on 23 July 1942 to become a prisoner of war. (Via P. Sikora)

on the Irving leather jacket and then the crunching walk across the iron-hard airfield to 'B's' dispersal. Then into the harsh glare of the bare electric light bulbs of the Nissen hut, grunt a sort of 'wot ho' to whoever happened to be there, and, picking up one's brolly [parachute], amble across the 200 yards of frosted grass and mud to [Spitfire] DW-P.

"Hoist brolly on to port wingtip to sit there with the straps hanging down, and then attempt to climb up on to the port wing root. I've sometimes taken four or five attempts before my foot would remain on the slippery, icy wing long enough for my frantic grabs to hold on to the windscreen armoured glass panel, the only hand-hold there was. Once stable on the wing, it was then a simple matter of pushing down the release button in the top centre of the hood, and to slide the hood back. Then reach in to the door release handle, and open the door out and down. Climb in, feet on seat, and, moving feet on to the foot slides, sit right down with a bump into the parachute well of the seat.

"First, on with a cockpit light – for night flying I never used the cockpit lights to ensure my night vision wasn't upset and did everything by feel. Check the reflector gun sight was set to 250 yard range and 60ft span (60ft

was about right for heavy stuff and made sure that for 109s I'd be a lot closer than 250 yards). Helmet placed over gun sight, with the oxygen tube plugged into the socket just below the ident switch control box on the right hand side (the socket was a bayonet), and the radio lead jack into the socket just in front of the seat.

"Check mixture lever right back, propeller pitch lever at fully fine, throttle right back, brakes on, gun button set to 'safe', both fuel levers up to off, and tail and rudder trims set for take-off. Align compass grid lines with needle ensuring 'red on red' so as not to fly in the opposite direction to that desired and then uncage [unlock] the D.I. [directional indicator gyro] and set it to agree with the compass and re-cage it. Check fuel tanks full, oxygen full and on, air and brake pressures at recommended level, radiator control lever at fully open, undercarriage signal sticks up out of the wing and green lights on.

"Place the four harness straps to be instantly available and not snagged on anything and then switch off the light, get out, shut the door and hood, and slide off the wing and wander back to dispersal to slump into a wicker armchair and catnap gently away until 9am with flying boots up on the cast-iron stove along with those of the other hopefuls …

"We were told the intention was to 'wake up' the *Luftwaffe* in France, who apparently were having an easy life having stopped the daylight

---

Left: Squadron Leader Piotr Laguna. A pre-war Polish Air Force pilot, Laguna escaped to France after the German invasion and flew with the *Armée de l'Air*, the French Air Force. Following a second German attack, the Blitzkrieg in 1940, he escaped to Britain, joining 302 Squadron for the Battle of Britain. He became Commanding Officer of 302 Squadron on 31 December 1940, succeeding Squadron Leader Mieczyslaw Mümler. Laguna was killed in action whilst leading the Northolt Wing on 27 June 1941, his Spitfire, P8331, being hit by ground fire. (Via P. Sikora)

attacks over here. Specifically, it was to be the 109s we were to upset, and I think it was probably Hamlyn (secure in his Battle of Britain reputation) who asked 'Why bother, it was nice and peaceful as it was'.

"The waking up was to take two forms. Small raids of two fighters per raid would dash across and out again shooting up anything to take their fancy; these would be known as 'mosquitoes'. Alternatively heavily escorted bombing raids on airports, railways etc. would, it was hoped, fetch the 109s up to be dealt with. This was the start of the large raids that took place through 1941. The first was in mid-January, but I wasn't on it. Up to 5th February, we didn't carry out a 'Mosquito' and later these became known as 'Rhubarbs'.

"Anyway, I was on readiness on the morning of 5th February 1941, and mid-morning the commanding officer popped his head into 'B' Flight to say 'released from 13.00 to 09.00 tomorrow morning'. As we all gave vent to various sounds of appreciation, he then smiled and said, 'that's after we get back from St Omer, take-off 12.00'.

"Then followed a fairly basic briefing – quite unlike those I've read of in its simplicity. We would follow 302 to Rye, climb up through the 10/10th cloud to about 15,000ft and join up with seven (I think) other fighter squadrons, where we would be top but one (having Tangmere's 65 above us). The whole shooting match would then escort twelve Blenheims to St Omer where they would cause great alarm and despondency with their 250lb bombs. 610 would fly in three vics, each of three aircraft, with Green Section slipping into the boxes.

"We went for lunch at 11.30 hours and after this I walked out to 'P' (DW-P) and asked my rigger to top the tanks up after he'd completed his pre-op engine run. He knew full well why I'd asked; as weaver I would use an awful lot of fuel and we only had about 1¾ hours of endurance at the best …[4]

"After checking 'P', it was back to dispersal to empty out pockets and to hear any last minute instructions. Incidentally, some three weeks

Above: Groundcrew from 610 (County of Chester) Squadron lark about with a cement mixer at Westhampnett. It was during late 1940 and early 1941, after the airfield had been turned into a quagmire, that the airfield's perimeter tracks and dispersals were improved and concreted. (610 (County of Chester) Squadron Association)

previously we all had to hand in our working tunics, and when they were returned each had an escape silk map sewn into a shoulder and a compass needle threaded on a cotton sewn into one of the front seams. Naturally we had to search for them, and to look at them. Consequently, our sewing was hardly as neatly done and I do remember thinking that only an idiot would think there was nothing wrong with one of my shoulders; it was lumpy …

"The commanding officer's Merlin coughed into life, and, almost immediately, the other eleven engines were adding their share to the noise and slipstream. Then section-by-section we all lurched over to near 'A' Flight dispersal, formed up and took off towards Chichester cathedral in the south-west.

"As we flew out the commanding officer ordered Green to go into the box – Green 1 and 2 were now rear of Red and Yellow sections respectively. It wasn't the most comfortable of formations; we were following 302, who had taken off just before us, [and] were about 1 mile behind and at a pedestrian 160 mph rather than our normal 180 mph everything felt most sloppy (302 were flying Hurricanes).

"The commanding officer told us to keep close and to climb to 15,000ft, so into and up through the murk we went; the cloud base was at about 1,500 feet and it was solid up to around 12,000 feet. I suppose twelve propellers must have churned it up well, for I could see all Blue Section quite easily, and caught glimpses of Red 3 beyond. Quick glances at my

Left: An aerial photograph taken in late 1940 which reveals that Westhampnett's perimeter track was just that – a rough track around the airfield. At this stage Westhampnett is still very basic, consisting of little more than a few dispersals and timber-framed buildings. The dark lines across the airfield are a basic form of camouflage, in which tar was poured on to the grass to create hedges or the outline of a building, added to deceive prying *Luftwaffe* aircraft. (Airfield Research Group)

A member of 610 (County of Chester) Squadron's groundcrew, Alf Bridson, is pictured with one of 'A' Flight's Spitfires, in this case that coded 'DW-A'. The white band on the rear of the fuselage was introduced in December 1940 to signify that the aircraft was a day fighter. Note the tented accommodation in the rear of the photograph, which was taken on the eastern boundary near Fishers Cottage looking north, that was used by groundcrew. (Author's Collection)

panel showed a nice easy climb so I relaxed hoping Red 1 would not become disorientated!

"We broke into brilliant sunshine and climbed to our Angels 15, by which time we were orbiting Rye waiting for the off. The strange thing was I could see no aircraft above us, and weirdly the cloud over England ended at the coast in an almost vertical cliff edge to leave the skies over the Channel and France completely cloudless. The Channel to the east looked ridiculously narrow, and the skies over the snow-clad French landscape were broodingly ominous.

"As usual, the sun glare blinding out of the clear blue made looking to the south-east difficult. God only knew what nasties were moving into its hidey-hole, and as we circled Rye for a good five minutes at least we certainly gave them plenty of time get ready for us. I guess, like me, that the others had their gun-sights switched 'on', their gun firing buttons turned to 'fire' and their hoods slid back for better visibility – and I bet they were sweating cobs too.

"Eventually, as we seemed to fly more or less in an easterly direction, the commanding officer gave the order 'Elfin aircraft – search formation – weavers go', and I, like Pilot Officer Fenwick behind Yellow Section, moved to be about 100 feet above Blue Section and just behind, and commenced swinging backwards and forwards across them in a series of elongated 'S' turns as we made towards Boulogne. I still couldn't see 65 Squadron above us, although they could have been outside my arc of vision. However, from what Pilot Officer Hill later told me, only his section turned up intact after climbing up through the cloud and was the only 65 formation to sit where they should have been.

"Weaving was quite energetic. The extent of my 'beat' was from just to port of Blue 3 across to almost behind Red 3, as we were in search formation with aircraft about four spans apart this would be about 100 yards, or a fraction more. Starting from the left-hand side I would fly angled across to the right-hand side, searching up and down to the rear as I did so. At the right hand side there would be a quick glance down to check I was still positioned safely above Green Section (approaching this point I would have already made sure I and Green 2 were not on a collision course), and then a steep left hand turn to get me on the outward trip when once again I would be searching to the rear. Then a steep right hand turn and start the cycle all over again … and so on, and so on.

"In retrospect there wasn't much time for searching, due to the need to be continually steep turning and checking position. I have since felt it would have been better to have had one aircraft weaving above and the other below, for then the beat would have been over some 250 yards giving a far longer search time. The weavers were known as 'arse-end Charleys', sometimes more politely 'tail-end Charleys'. At the end we most certainly were, and we must have been Charleys to get stuck with the job! Of course the other ten aircraft had a far quieter time – flying straight and level and looking only inwards so they could keep position with the section leader and watch for trouble at the same time.

"Just after crossing the French coast I reported some contrails up to port and slightly to our rear, but they extinguished almost immediately, so whatever it was had moved either above or below the contrail level. I had no idea where we were.

"There was no time to look at the map which was left folded in my left boot – but we must have been near to the target (the airfield at St Omer). I caught a flash way up behind as I was about to start the steep turn back

Opposite: Sergeant John Hayley, on the left, and a colleague work on the propeller of one of 610 (County of Chester) Squadron's aircraft. They are standing in the opening of a canvas hangar that was erected in a field outside the airfield's boundary to the south-east. The groundcrew had to push aircraft through a gap in the hedge on the boundary to reach this hangar. (610 (County of Chester) Squadron Association)

towards the centre once more. I held off the turn to have a good check, and then turned back, only to see the squadron a good 800 yards or so away in front as my extended run had taken us apart. As speed in regaining position seemed to be vital – it was not clever to be on one's own in enemy skies – I did a quick left and right steep turn during which I had a good shufti behind, and then slung the coal on and went fast to get back with the rest.

"I was about halfway back, and about to have another look behind, when there was a sudden staccato vibration and sparks seemed to erupt out of my port wingtip. 'Bloody hell'. A steep left-hand turn initiation only just beat a violent clang from up front, at which the rudder pedals suddenly lost all feel and became seemingly disconnected from the rudder. As the nose fell away the cockpit filled with a white mist accompanied by a foul smell of glycol and 100-octane fuel. I let the nose go on down hoping whatever it was couldn't follow and that the mist would clear before it became a problem.

"The mist rapidly went however, and I was able to ease out of the steep diving turn to edge slightly west of north whilst weaving like mad one way and the other to clear my tail, and able now to check damage. The port wingtip was mangled, the rudder just a useless uncontrollable flap, the radiator and oil temperatures were perhaps a little too high, and the elevator perhaps a bit less than precise. However she was still flying and I was at about 9,000ft having lost the rest in the diving turn, and thinking it might be an uncomfortable ride home.

"Over the next few minutes the radiator and oil temperature showed a gradual but steady rise, and I found the cause of the petrol smell; nearly twenty gallons of fuel were sloshing about in the belly of the fuselage under my feet. I now knew why my lower legs were so cold on the ground. I later found the insides of my flying boot and my trouser legs were absolutely saturated with the damn stuff. On checking the fuel gauge the top tank was empty so that had clearly been hit, as had the glycol tank or piping.

"By now I had to accept a gradual height loss in order to maintain the 290mph desirable as the Merlin seemed not to be giving its best. Another cause of disquiet was the ever-increasing amount of tail heavy trim having to be wound on to stop the nose from dropping. Looking in my rear view mirror I thought I could see strips of fabric trailing from the elevators, [though] the view was not all that clear.

"Some six minutes after being hit we were down to maybe 6,000ft with the radiator temp. almost in the red. I could see the Channel – and had seen the Blenheims pass about 1,000ft above me clearly on their way home and going like the Devil.

"My thought was that she'd never reach the Channel and I wasn't about to try to put her down – not with all that petrol washing around, so like a good Boy Scout I prepared by disconnecting my helmet leads and ramming them securely into my parachute harness straps, and then released my Sutton harness so I was unattached to the aircraft. There seemed little point in doing anything else as I'd run out of scope in playing with pitch control and throttle, and when all throttle movement had been used she was clearly going to go in only one direction, even if the overheating didn't do it first … and that was down.

"I decided to stand on the seat and then kick the stick forward to throw me out, but my planning came to naught. A most expensive sounding noise came from up front, accompanied by darkish smoke and jets of flame, and as I started to stand, letting go of the stick, dear old 'P' helped me to the last. She threw her nose violently down and I shot up and out like the cork from a bottle!

"And then there was only a flickering jumble of sky and snow as I

Opposite: The same propeller as in the previous image is now being fitted to the Spitfire using very basic facilities – oil drums and step ladders – and brute force. (610 (County of Chester) Squadron Association)

obviously somersaulted, until I yanked the ripcord. What a relief to be right way up, and even greater to look up and check the beautiful white canopy fully open. My right boot had disappeared as I was launched from the aircraft, so the landing itself – on one foot to save my unbooted one – was a bit of a thud, but there I was in the middle of a snow-covered stubble field [which was] iron hard!

"The only cover in sight was a clump of bushes maybe 100 yards away up a slight slope. They were not leafed and even a mouse would have laughed at them, but I couldn't be a chooser so I dragged myself and chute up there, where there was snow about eighteen inches deep into which I pushed the chute and the mike from my helmet. I then attempted to 'shoe' my right foot by tying the oxygen tube in such a fashion as to hold the helmet around my foot; this worked reasonably well.

"I was now aware I hadn't had a pee since early in the morning, and I was thus engaged, crouched behind these silly little bushes, when two uniforms walked through a field entrance some 250 yards away. I finished my pee lying down! It was to no avail, they walked straight up to me, and, as I stood up, the one with the gun said, 'For you the war is over' – and I thought they only said that in things like the 'Hotspur' and 'Magnet' – we live and learn.

"It was all very friendly, and we walked as a small group down to the opening they'd come through, meeting on the way a French boy of about

---

Left: An aerial view of the entrance to Westhampnett airfield taken in 1941. This is in the north-east corner of the airfield adjacent to the Officers' Mess at Woodcote Farm. The building numbered (1) is the cookhouse; (2) is the CO's office and the Orderly Room; (3) the Engineer's Office; (4) the Guard Room; (5) Woodcote Farmhouse; (6) the Officers' Mess; (7) the Aerodrome; (8) the road to Lavant; (9) the road to Chichester; and (10) the road to Goodwood. (610 (County of Chester) Squadron Association)

eight years old who asked my age. Although I understood him perfectly my answer of twenty-one was given using all eight fingers and two thumbs twice and a bit!

"We got into the Ford V8 they'd arrived in, and drove, perhaps, 400 yards to where the remains of poor 'P' were smoking. She had impacted on the side of the road which was sunken slightly below the field level, and all that could be seen was a rather buckled tail assembly sitting on top of a mass of jumbled scrap metal in what was clearly a damn great hole. I could see nothing identifiable in this mess – no sign of seat, panel, oxygen bottles – no nothing; and I guessed it was my good fortune not to be with it all umpteen feet down.

"Broken chunks of mainplane lay at the side together with the broken remains of eight Browning .303 machine-guns, barrels snapped, and eight ammo boxes with sides peeled back to show the indentations of the cartridge rims on the inside surfaces looking most like a machined finish. Ammunition lay everywhere. Loose wreckage lay all over the road and I picked up the tail wheel from 200 yards inside an adjacent field!

"Leaving 'P' to her lonely roadside grave … we drove to the airfield at St Omer, barely ten minutes away and I was decamped outside what looked like a haystack but which was in fact a building. The adjacent hut disgorged a load of about twelve *Luftwaffe* pilots, who, one by one, came to attention in front of me and then saluted. Of course I had to reciprocate. At that time there was a fair degree of mutual respect between us, mirroring that of the First World War.

"Anyway I was treated with extreme courtesy and had my own personal guide appointed – an English-speaking pilot recovering from a perforated eardrum. In the crew room I was introduced to the pilot who shot me down, *Major* Oesau, who became one of the top scoring pilots before losing his life in 1944. We spoke for a couple of minutes with my escort as interpreter, and then I signed his cigarette case in pencil for him to have engraved over.

"There were six other English names there from, I should think, the battle in France in 1940. After I'd turned out my pockets, ignoring the two letters mentioned earlier, I was taken on a tour of their part of St Omer airfield. We went to a clothing store where he gave me a brand new German flying boot for my right foot. He wouldn't make it the pair, so from then until we marched out of Fallingbostel in 1945 I wore odd flying boots!

"Returning to the crew room, I met Pilot Officer Hill who had been in the sole 65 Squadron section to get into place … Later, when we were on our own, he said the 109s went through their section as if they weren't there, and then doubtless down on to us! He had some cannon shell splinters in his back and was somewhat sore. He didn't know what had happened to the other three, but was not too hopeful.

"They transferred us to the pilots' quarters in a large, old country house about ten minutes' drive away. This was the Abbey Notre Dame at Wisques. Next day it was off to Germany and Poland for a journey around the PoW camps."[5]

During February 1941, 610 Squadron changed its Spitfires to the Mk.IIa variant. It was mainly involved in standing patrols along the South Coast along with the occasional interception. However, it was back on offensive sweeps by the end of the month.

Early March saw two brothers, Australians Pilot Officer Frederick 'Tony' Gaze and Pilot Officer Irvine Scott Gaze, posted to the squadron. Tony became a successful fighter pilot who would be instrumental in the initiation of motor racing at Goodwood. Irvine Gaze, however, did not survive long, being killed whilst on patrol. His brother later recalled Irvine's fate: "We were all flying in very low cloud expecting Ju 88 and Do 217 intruders popping out of the cloud and bombing. I made sure I was over the sea before breaking cloud and found we had two aircraft missing after landing, including Scott's."[6]

The squadron landed at Westhampnett hoping that both missing aircraft would return. Whist one did, a pall of smoke coming from behind the South Downs indicated the fate of the other. Scott's Spitfire had crashed at West Dean.

April saw 610 Squadron undertake some bomber escorts to France but no enemy aircraft were encountered. May saw the airfield becoming busier, as well as the arrival of 616 (South Yorkshire) Squadron on 9 May. Whilst its CO was Squadron Leader Howard 'Billy' Burton, 616 brought with it Wing Commander Douglas Bader, who was the Tangmere Wing Leader at the time. On 29 August 1941, 610 Squadron left Westhampnett, being posted to Leconfield.

As operations intensified during the spring of 1941, 616 (South Yorkshire) Squadron came to terms with its new home. Its ORB mentions that "although the accommodation is not quite so good for all concerned, the change is for the better".[7]

With the limited accommodation available at Westhampnett having reached bursting point, some of the officers were also accommodated at Shopwyke House, just to the west of Tangmere, whilst a few made 'Rushmans', a property in nearby Oving, their residence. Douglas Bader and his wife, Thelma, resided at 'Bay House' near Bognor, where many of the pilots often went for recreation after flying.

Another auxiliary squadron, 616 had moved south to Tangmere in early 1941. It was during the early stages of this transfer that, on 18 March, Wing Commander Douglas Bader, previously of 242 Squadron, arrived to take command of the three Spitfire squadrons of the Tangmere Wing – Nos. 145, 610 and 616, which were then based at Merston, Westhampnett and Tangmere respectively. He always led 616 in his personal Spitfire with the code letters 'DB', flying with it right through to his final operation over France on 9 August 1941.

Amongst the squadron's sergeant pilots was Alan Smith. Much to Smith's surprise, he was selected to fly as the Wing Leader's wingman: "Wing Commander Douglas Bader arrived and announced that he would be flying with 616 and had decided that Red Section would consist of himself, 'Cocky' Dundas, 'Johnnie' Johnson and myself, Sergeant Pilot Alan Smith. I need hardly say I was surprised and delighted!"[8] In fact, Smith served as Bader's wingman right through to the day the latter was shot down – though Smith was not flying as he was suffering from a cold. On this particular day, his position had been filled by Jeff West, another sergeant pilot on the squadron.

Sergeant Alan Smith, later Flight Lieutenant Alan Smith DFC & Bar, DL, was a staunch fan of Douglas Bader. The youngest son of Captain Alfred Smith, Alan was born at South Shields, County Durham, on 14 March 1917. After his father had been lost at sea, he left school at the age of 14 to help his mother in her ironmongery store. He wrote to the RAF in 1939 explaining his education had been curtailed and making it clear that he would be willing to attend night school to do everything he could to reach the required standard to become a pilot. He joined the RAFVR and attended lectures in the town centre three nights a week on technical subjects.

Smith began his training on the Tiger Moth in the spring of 1939, and flew the Spitfire for the first time at No.7 Operational Training Unit (OTU). He was initially sent to 610 (County of Chester) Squadron in October 1940, before being posted to 616 (South Yorkshire) Squadron in December of that year.

He recalls the day he first encountered the legendary flyer: "We had just

Right: Some of 610 Squadron's groundcrew in front of one of its Spitfires at Westhampnett in early 1941. Corporal Ted Phenna is the individual kneeling on the right of the front row. (610 (County of Chester) Squadron Association)

come back from an operation and were at readiness, refuelling and such like, when a single Spitfire flew across the airfield, and performed aerobatics, the like of which you had never seen. It did three slow rolls, flick rolls and side-slipped down to a perfect landing beautifully, like a butterfly. He [the pilot] switched off and the prop stopped.

"The hood slid back and out got this legless guy we had heard about. He came into the dispersal hut and said, 'I am Douglas Bader and I have come to take over the Wing. I have decided to fly with 616 Squadron.' All other Wing Commanders took turns to fly with all their squadrons, but Douglas looked around those standing in the hut and he saw Billy Burton, Cocky Dundas, and spoke to each of them in turn. Then he spoke with Johnnie Johnson, who he had obviously heard of.

"He looked at me and said, 'Who are you'? I replied, 'I'm Sergeant Smith sir'. He said to me 'You'll do – you can fly as my number two.' Needless to say I was taken aback. I was just an ordinary sergeant pilot. I can't say that I flew with him on all trips but most. He was a great leader."[9]

Bader's section of four aircraft used the call sign "Dogsbody". The wing commander's only comment on choosing Smith was: "God help you if you let any Hun get on my tail."

Left: Ground staff work on a 610 (County of Chester) Squadron Spitfire Mk.V at Westhampnett, 11 April 1943. Corporal Maurice Houseman (on top of the cowling), Corporal Ted Phenna (holding the oil can) and Sergeant Moore (working on the main wheels) had all been with the squadron since its formation in February 1936. (IWM; CH9248)

Opposite: Spitfire 'DW-A' with some of 'A' Flight's groundcrew on the eastern boundary during the winter of 1941. In the back row, standing left to right, are Alf Bridson and Stan Rogers; sitting in the middle is Steve Biggs; whilst in the front row are Robbie Robinson and Sid Cogan. (610 (County of Chester) Squadron Association)

Another member of the section, Johnnie Johnson, once described Smith as "a perfect number two who never lost sight of his leader".[10] For his part, Smith recalled Johnson with affection: "Johnnie was everyone's pal; Johnnie enjoyed life and he was a bloody good pilot. In all the war, he only once had a bullet hole in his aeroplane. He was a damn good shot because he had spent much of his youth shooting partridges. He knew deflection shooting, far better than townsfolk like me who had never fired a gun in my life."

Westhampnett was ideal also for those wanting to play golf, as recounted by Johnnie Johnson: "Sometimes when the wing was released to one hour's availability, Bader, the CO, Ken and one of the other squadron commanders made up a foursome and played golf on the rolling Goodwood course. Occasionally I caddied for him and was astonished to see the accuracy and strength with which he smacked them down the fairway. When he addressed the ball on the tee, his powerful arms flexed and a look of grim determination appeared on his face – it was if he could see a little 109 perching on the peg instead of the inoffensive white ball.

"Back at Westhampnett a pilot stood by the ops [operations] telephone and outside our hut was our little Maggie [Miles Magister]. Should the wing be called to readiness, the pilot would jump into the cockpit, fly low over the golf course, which was but a mile or two away, and fire off a red Very light. One of our party (Pilot Officer Johnson) would race to the clubhouse, start the wing commander's car and drive across the course to collect the rest of the party. We estimated we could be back at Westhampnett within half an hour of the recall message."[11]

Throughout the summer of 1941 the pilots of the Tangmere Wing ranged across northern France, often on *Rhubarb* and *Circus* operations. As ever, these sorties were not without danger or mishaps.

In early June, for example, one of 610 Squadron's Spitfires, that flown by Pilot Officer Sutherland RCAF, struck a tree when coming in to land after a local practice flight. The aircraft was a write-off; Sutherland damaged his spine. Pilot Officer Thomas Leckie RNZAF was the next to suffer such an indignity when, on 18 June, he overshot the runway at Westhampnett as he was landing. His aircraft turned over; the serious injuries Leckie sustained meant he was unable to fly for several months.

It was also at about this time that pilots of the United States Army Air Force (USAAF) were being attached to RAF squadrons for experience and familiarisation. One such individual, Lieutenant Montgomery, joined 616 Squadron for a week at the end of June 1941.

In what Johnnie Johnson came to describe as "The High Summer", under Bader's leadership the Tangmere Wing's successes soon mounted. Smith recalls how his role was not to rack up his own tally. He also remembers that Bader would often make calls over the radio to calm his pilots down during stressful periods:

"My job was to watch his tail and watch out for the Hun in the sun. I was to cling to him like a limpet. No one can describe what it's like to be in the middle of an air combat. One minute flying along in perfect formation, blue sky and peaceful and sun shining, then all of a sudden all Hell breaks loose. I called it a beehive – aircraft going in all directions. Then all of a sudden nothing, everything vanishes.

"We didn't have time to be frightened really, but you were on edge. In the middle of all this action, aircraft exploding and parachutes opening all around. You would suddenly hear Bader calling up Group Captain Woodhall on the radio, he was the Tangmere Sector controller, and say

Opposite: Groundcrew from 610 (County of Chester) Squadron pose in front of one of the tents used for their accommodation, though as well as living in tents, some of them took up residence in the Duke's hangar across the road. (610 (County of Chester) Squadron Association)

Left: Another group of 610 (County of Chester) Squadron groundcrew gather for a photograph, though this time in front of Spitfire 'DW-B', with the South Downs and the Trundle in the background. (610 (County of Chester) Squadron Association)

Opposite: Arthur Holford, a member of 610 (County of Chester) Squadron's groundcrew, rests on the side of the cockpit of Spitfire Mk.II P7923. Coded 'DW-H' and named *Venture I*, this presentation aircraft arrived at the squadron on 25 February 1941, being re-allocated to 130 Squadron in July of that year. A sister aircraft, P7924, was named *Venture II* and served with 145 Squadron. Note the dispersal huts being erected in the background. (610 (County of Chester) Squadron Association)

'Woody old chap, Douglas here. I quite forgot to book a squash court for 7 o'clock, can you book one for me?' All of a sudden there was an aura of peace around you as you digested the fact that if Douglas was not afraid, what was I doing being afraid?"[12]

Smith also remembered one event which typified Bader's approach to leadership. When the military police tried to arrest some of the Tangmere Wing's pilots for using aviation fuel in their motor cars, Bader jumped to their support:

"We all had little old rusty motor cars and I had a 1932 MG midget with a spare wheel on the back. Many of us had these little cars and we filled them with aviation fuel. One lunchtime we were hanging round at readiness and the military police came around and started testing the fuel in the cars. They found a number with aviation fuel and were going to arrest us all!

"A car pulled up and out climbs Bader who stomped across saying, 'What the hell's going on here?' The military policeman tried to explain what was happening, that we had broken all the rules. Bader started on

Above: Sergeant Woodrow 'Bill' Raine takes a turn to pose in *Venture I* – note the sailing ship emblem on a yellow patch above the nickname. Deflectors have been fitted in front of the cockpit to reduce glare from the exhaust ports during night flying. Raine was posted to 610 (County of Chester) Squadron on 5 October 1940. He remained with the squadron throughout the early offensive operations over northern Europe, clocking up two Bf 109s destroyed and two probables before being shot down and killed in Spitfire Vb 'DW-P' on 21 August 1941. The same squadron code letters were carried on his best friend's, David Denchfield's, aircraft when he, Denchfield, had been shot down several months previously. (Woodrow Raine, via the late David Denchfield)

this chap and cut him down. 'Get your buggers out of here, and fast, or I will sort you out'. Well those are my words, but you can imagine what he said. We never heard any more about it."[13]

Smith recalled that Bader flew as often as he could: "He was never out of the cockpit. He was such a great pilot. I think eventually he was getting tired and could have done with a rest. He always insisted on flying on every operation. I always enjoyed flying with him and I always managed to stay with him in combat. I was too scared to leave him!

"He drove himself very hard – harder than he expected anyone else to work. I learned all my skills from him. As we crossed the coast on the way back from France he would get you to tuck in close in formation – you felt safe with him as he was the wing commander. He would often beckon me closer, very close in behind his wing. You could see him in the cockpit sucking on his pipe as we crossed back over the English coast.

"He was quite a colourful character. It used to be amusing that once a week that he would get a signal asking for him to 'moderate his language in the air' as the WAAFs were refusing to write down what he said! On one occasion – I wasn't there – the story goes that he went to the cinema and asked the ice cream girl, 'Miss can you get me a screwdriver'. She promptly did; he undid a few screws and took his legs off and she subsequently fainted!"

On 9 August 1941, Bader and Squadron Leader Buck Casson AFC, DFC, were lost in action. Both survived and were taken prisoner.

Bader had lost one of his false legs when he was shot down and the Germans offered free passage to an RAF aircraft to drop a replacement near St Omer, where he was being held. The RAF refused, preferring to help Bader on its own terms. Consequently, a few days it later mounted a bombing operation during which a new false leg was dropped by parachute. Smith was one of the pilots that escorted the Blenheim bombers on the mission: "I can still remember seeing the box dropping under the parachute; it was one hell of a day, low broken cloud and rain. We had six Blenheims, the weather was appalling and the bombers could not drop their bombs on the target at Lille, but the leg was dropped over St Omer."

After Bader's loss the Tangmere Wing was taken over by Wing Commander S.A.H. 'Tony' Woodhouse who had previously flown with the Americans in 71 (Eagle) Squadron and then with 610 Squadron. Reflecting on his first Wing Leader, Smith said: "Douglas was an enormous personality and very old school tie, either in or out of prison as he was either hated or loved! What I loved about Bader was that he didn't like administrative officers; he was a man to get things done. A great guy and I was privileged to fly with him."

An important day for 610 Squadron during its time at Westhampnett came on 26 August 1941, when it was presented with its crest which had been approved by the King. Air Marshall Leigh-Mallory flew down specifically to carry out the presentation. The following day, the squadron departed for Leconfield.

Operationally, September was a quiet month, due, to a large degree, to extremely poor weather. Rain and low cloud meant that 616 Squadron was

Right: Pilot Officer Frederick Anthony Owen 'Tony' Gaze in the cockpit of his Spitfire at Westhampnett. Tony Gaze and his brother, Scott, were both posted to 610 (County of Chester) Squadron in March 1941. Tony achieved his first 'kill' in Spitfire 'DW-H' on 26 June that year. Having taken off from Westhampnett on 23 March 1941, Scott was killed whilst pursuing a German raider in cloud. He is buried in Chichester. Tony Gaze went on to be credited with eleven kills, with three shared destroyed, four probables and five damaged, and was awarded the DFC and two Bars. Post-war he became a successful racing driver and in fact was instrumental in suggesting that Westhampnett's perimeter track could be used for motor racing. (610 (County of Chester) Squadron Association)

to complete only seven offensive sweeps over northern France. Then, on 20 September, Hugh Dundas was posted out of 616 Squadron, to an OTU. He had been one of the original members of the squadron, his service dating back to the Battle of Britain, but, having done over sixty sweeps across the Channel, it was felt that he needed a rest. However, it was not long before he returned to Westhampnett, this time flying a Hawker Typhoon with 56 Squadron in 1942.

Another disaster befell the Westhampnett-based squadrons, and more specifically 616 Squadron, on 22 September 1941. During a practice attack Pilot Officer Edwin Burton RCAF, who was leading a section, broke left sharply and collided with Sergeant J.B. Slack. Both aircraft were seen to crash into the Channel about one mile south of Brighton Pier. Neither pilot survived. Burton had only just returned from leave and had announced his engagement; Slack was recently married.

A new CO was posted in to 616 Squadron at the end of September, in the form of Squadron Leader Colin Gray DFC & Bar, replacing Squadron Leader Burton. However, the unit had come to the end of its time at Westhampnett and was posted north to Kirton Lindsey on 5 October 1941.

Left: Alf Bridson pictured in front of a 610 (County of Chester) Squadron Mk.II Spitfire, that coded 'DW-K', in early 1941. (610 (County of Chester) Squadron Association)

Right: Sergeant Herbert David Denchfield with his best friend Sergeant Woodrow Raine at the rear of Fishers Cottage, the sergeants' accommodation at Westhampnett. Denchfield joined 610 (County of Chester) Squadron on 7 October 1940, just in time for the end of the Battle of Britain. (Woodrow Raine, via the late David Denchfield)

Below Right: A view of Sergeant Samuel Hamer, and two fellow pilots, with his Spitfire, coded 'DW-N', which was believed to have been taken in February 1941. (Woodrow Raine, via the late David Denchfield)

Below: Sergeant Samuel Hamer is the pilot of this Spitfire, which was photographed from 610 (County of Chester) Squadron's hack – a Miles Magister – somewhere over the Sussex countryside. (Woodrow Raine, via the late David Denchfield)

Opposite: A group photograph of 610 (County of Chester) Squadron personnel taken on Westhampnett's southern boundary, looking north, in July 1941. Sitting in the back row, left to right, are Pilot Officer Tony Gaze, Sergeant Doley, Sergeant Ballard, Pilot Officer Grey, Pilot Officer Stoop, and Sergeant Phillpotts. The middle row comprises Pilot Officer Bartholomew, Flying Officer Lloyd, Flying Officer le Fleming, Flight Lieutenant Lee Knight, Squadron Leader Ken Holden (the CO), Flight Lieutenant Milling, Pilot Officer More, Flying Officer Higson and Pilot Officer Hugill. Sitting in the front row, meanwhile, are Sergeant McWatt, Sergeant Main, Sergeant Wright, Sergeant Richardson, Sergeant Raine and Sergeant Day. An indication of the actual date the picture was taken can be gleaned from the knowledge that Wright was posted to the squadron on 13 July, whilst Bartholomew was posted out the following day. (610 (County of Chester) Squadron Association)

Right: Aircraftman John Anderson at Initial Training Wing, Torquay prior to his flying training. John subsequently joined 616 (South Yorkshire) Squadron at Westhampnett, only to be almost immediately posted across to 610 (County of Chester) Squadron. After only a few sorties, Anderson was shot down during *Circus* 42 on 10 July 1941. Despite being wounded in the leg, he managed to ditch his Spitfire and climb into his dinghy. After many hours he was rescued by a German E-boat. His best friend, Sergeant Horace Blackman, who was on the same operation, was not so lucky, being shot down and killed. The other pilot lost as a result of enemy action that day was Flight Lieutenant Peter Ward Smith, from 610 Squadron, who also became a PoW. John survived his captivity and ended up being one of the unfortunate participants of the 'Long March'. (John Anderson)

Right: Sergeant Samuel Hamer standing in front of his aircraft at dispersal in the winter of 1940/1941. As can be gauged from this image, the condition of the airfield at Westhampnett during this period was somewhat poor. At the controls of Spitfire Mk.II P7501, Hamer was attacked whilst participating in *Circus* 6 on 5 March 1941, this being a raid on Boulogne Dock, which was heavily opposed by aircraft from *JG*51 and I(J)/*LG*2. With his aircraft having been hit in the wings and fuselage by cannon fire, Hamer was killed trying to crash-land at Wilmington, Sussex. His aircraft was repaired. (Woodrow Raine, via the late David Denchfield)

Left: Sergeant (later Sir) Alan Smith with his car, nicknamed *Fear Not*, at dispersal on the eastern boundary at Westhampnett looking north. Both Tony Gaze and Alan Smith recalled having their cars at the airfield and driving around the perimeter track. (The late Alan Smith)

Above: The Commanding Officer of 616 (South Yorkshire) Squadron, Billy Burton (on the left), with the Earl of Titchfield outside 'B' Flight's dispersal hut in July 1941. (G.R. Pitchfork Collection)

Right: Sergeant Pilot Alan Smith climbing out of his Spitfire, a picture which was taken whilst he was serving with 610 (County of Chester) Squadron between October and December 1940. His first claim for an enemy aircraft occurred with 616 (South Yorkshire) Squadron during a sortie in the Lille area on 2 July 1940; he shot down a Bf 109E, and damaged a further one, whilst flying Spitfire Mk.II P8369, a presentation aircraft called *Toba*. (The late Alan Smith)

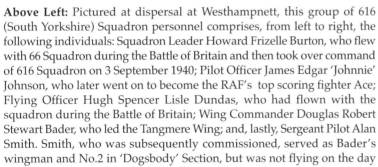

Above Left: Pictured at dispersal at Westhampnett, this group of 616 (South Yorkshire) Squadron personnel comprises, from left to right, the following individuals: Squadron Leader Howard Frizelle Burton, who flew with 66 Squadron during the Battle of Britain and then took over command of 616 Squadron on 3 September 1940; Pilot Officer James Edgar 'Johnnie' Johnson, who later went on to become the RAF's top scoring fighter Ace; Flying Officer Hugh Spencer Lisle Dundas, who had flown with the squadron during the Battle of Britain; Wing Commander Douglas Robert Stewart Bader, who led the Tangmere Wing; and, lastly, Sergeant Pilot Alan Smith. Smith, who was subsequently commissioned, served as Bader's wingman and No.2 in 'Dogsbody' Section, but was not flying on the day

that Bader was shot down whilst flying from Westhampnett on 9 August 1940. (The late Alan Smith)

Above Right: Another group of 616 (South Yorkshire) Squadron personnel at Westhampnett. To the right of 'Johnnie' Johnson, 'Cocky' Dundas and Douglas Bader is an American pilot posted to Westhampnett as an observer. (Alfred Price)

Opposite: Wing Commander Douglas Bader's personal aircraft, with its distinctive code letters 'DB', at Westhampnett. A Mk.IIa, P7966 was a presentation Spitfire called *Manxman*. (Alfred Price)

Above: The sergeants of 616 (South Yorkshire) Squadron's 'A' Flight at Woodcote Farm. Standing on top of the truck is Sergeant Ronald Leslie Brewer RNZAF, who was killed on 25 June 1941 whilst flying Spitfire P7327. Sitting to his right is Sergeant Alan Smith, Bader's usual wingman, whilst to his left is Sergeant Jeff West RNZAF, who was actually flying as Bader's stand-in wingman on the day he was shot down. The fourth individual, standing at the front, is Sergeant S.W.R. Mabbett. (The Andy Saunders Collection)

Right: Sergeant Alan Smith, on the left, with Flight Lieutenant Gibbs, 616 (South Yorkshire) Squadron's intelligence officer. (G.R. Pitchfork Collection)

Above: The pilots of the Tangmere Wing pictured at Westhampnett. Douglas Bader can be seen sat in the middle with his arms folded. He is surrounded by a mix of Nos. 145, 610 and 616 aircrew, including, to Bader's left, Squadron Leader Ken Holden (610 (County of Chester) Squadron) and, to Bader's right, Squadron Leader Stan Turner (145 Squadron). Behind Bader, and slightly to his left, is Tony Gaze of 610 Squadron. 'Nip' Heppell and 'Johnnie' Johnson are, respectively, to the right of and behind Turner. The wing was known as Bader's Bus Company. (Tangmere Military Aviation Museum)

Above: Sergeant Pilots of 616 (South Yorkshire) Squadron with, to the right, Leading Aircraftman Durham, outside the 'B' Flight hut at Westhampnett. (ww2images)

Above right: Four of 616 (South Yorkshire) Squadron's pilots at Westhampnett. From left to right they are Flight Lieutenant Colin MacFie, Flying Officer 'Cocky' Dundas (who is wearing a pre-war flying suit), Pilot Officer Phillip 'Nip' Heppell, and Pilot Officer 'Johnnie' Johnson. MacFie, who had flown with 611 (West Lancashire) Squadron during the Battle of Britain, became a PoW after being forced down on 5 July 1941. For his part,

Heppell was one of the first pilots to fly a Spitfire off the aircraft carrier HMS *Eagle*, to Malta, in 1942. (The Andy Saunders Collection)

Opposite: Squadron Leader Ken Holden (standing centre), the CO of 610 (County of Chester) Squadron, with a group of 'A' Flight pilots at Westhampnett. The others in the back row, from left to right, are: Sergeant McCairns, Pilot Office 'Nip' Heppell, 'Johnnie' Johnson and Sergeant S.W.R. Mabbett. The two men in the front row are Sergeant Jeff West RNZAF and Sergeant R. Brewer, another New Zealander. (The Andy Saunders Collection)

Above left: The grave of Sergeant Woodrow Raine, at St Omer Cemetery, pictured just after the war's end. (The late David Denchfield)

Above: Wing Commander Douglas Bader (fifth from left) and Flying Officer 'Cocky' Dundas (to Bader's immediate right) discussing the details of a sortie whilst walking back to dispersal. In the background can be seen Stoke Clump and The Trundle, both on the South Downs. Of interest is the fact that this photograph appears to be taken to the north of the road that runs to Lavant, indicating that much of the land surrounding the airfield proper was used for military purposes by the RAF. (The late Alan Smith)

Left: The pilots of 616 (South Yorkshire) Squadron's 'A' Flight at Westhampnett in June 1941. Standing in the back row, from left to right, are Johnson, Mabbett, Scott and McCairns, whilst in the front are Dundas, Hepple and Alan Smith. (G.R. Pitchfork Collection)

When 610 (County of Chester) Squadron departed RAF Westhampnett it was replaced by 129 (Mysore) Squadron which joined 616 (South Yorkshire) Squadron as part of the Tangmere Wing. Arriving on 29 August 1941, 129 Squadron had only been formed in June that year. Initially equipped with Spitfire Mk.Is, these were exchanged for Mk.Vbs after its arrival at Westhampnett.

The Commanding Officer at this stage was Squadron Leader Dennis Armitage DFC who had flown through the Battle of Britain with 266 Squadron.[1] Two of 129 Squadron's original pilots were Sergeant Ray Sherk and Sergeant Jimmy Whalen, both of whom were amongst six other NCO pilots from the RCAF. There were also two Australians and a pilot from Jamaica, whilst the remainder were from the RAF. Sherk described his arrival at Westhampnett:

"We were part of 12 Group and clearly preparing for a move forward to 11 Group – the 'sizzle' sector on the South Coast. We could hardly wait, but became apprehensive when it happened.

"We flew the squadron formation (12 Spitfires) and landed at Westhampnett to relieve 610 Squadron with whom we exchanged our Spitfires. They then flew back to Leconfield for a rest in our Mark I and II Spitfires; we had their Mark Vs with flush rivets, two 20mm cannon and four machine-guns. The very latest fighters!

"Air Marshal Leigh Mallory and Group Captain Beamish came to inspect us and said they had read our combat reports with interest. It didn't take long. I was on a sweep the next day to Le Treport but there was no action. On September 7th, [Sergeant P.] Boddy and [Pilot Officer] Cunliffe had a mid-air collision. Boddy baled out successfully, whilst Cunliffe made a successful force-landing back on the airfield at Westhampnett.

"Jim Whalen and I painted 'nose art' on our Spitfires on September the 10th 1941, his being a family crest and mine, on DV-X, a shooting star."[2]

Whalen, for his part, had a successful time at Westhampnett. He claimed three Bf 109s in this period, two of which were attacked on 17 September – as described by Whalen in a letter to his family in 1941:

"I was on a sweep leading Green Section when I saw a Bf 109F about to attack my number two. I turned after him and shot him down and then lost the squadron. I was going to head for England when I saw a squadron above, about ten to twenty miles inside France. I didn't know who they were so headed towards them. When I was close enough I saw they were Bf109 Es. About 12-15 flying in formation.

"I attacked and shot down the first Jerry. I missed the next then damaged a third, who might have crashed, and was going to shoot a fourth when my ammunition finished. I could see nothing but Jerrys about me and I beat it for England as fast as I could doing all kinds of queer manoeuvres to keep the 109s away from me."[3]

Ray Sherk remembers that there was not much rest for the squadron during its early days at Westhampnett: "We were in action almost every day until the end of October, by which time many of the original pilots had been lost or posted. The Commanding Officer, Squadron Leader Armitage, went down on the 21st September, along with my very good friend Lloyd MacDonald who was killed in action. Jim shot down his third Bf 109 on the same day as well as three more being confirmed as destroyed, one each to Tucker, Armstrong and Bowman.

"Tony Drew was also shot down in the air battle that day, he baled out and landed in the Channel where he was picked up by uninjured by the air sea rescue unit. Spence-Ross went down over Amiens on the 27th September and was posted missing in action. During this operation Hardy shot down an Me 109 and I missed one because I was out of range.

"One of my instructors, Flight Lieutenant Abrahams, arrived the next day as a Squadron Leader to replace Armitage as Commanding Officer.

Above: Spitfire Mk.Vs of 129 (Mysore) Squadron taking off from RAF Westhampnett, across the airfield from the south-west corner, around September 1941. No.129 Squadron was based at Westhampnett from August 1941 through to July 1942, with a short break at Debden. Note the water tower of Graylingwell Hospital in the background on the far right. (Courtesy of Ray Sherk)

We were busy doing convoy patrols, *Rhubarbs* and sweeps almost every day. Smith and Stuvinga were killed in a mid-air collision on the 5th of October while flying in formation led by Jim Whalen. Apparently Stuvinga flew in to Smith during a change to echelon starboard in cloud. Smith tried to bale out – too late. On the 7th Jim and I took the role of 109s doing 'snapper attacks' on the rest of the squadron flying in formation …

"About half the original pilots were still around in mid October and more would be gone in a few weeks. Pilot replacements kept arriving to fill the vacancies. It was exciting and adventuresome to say the least. Each of us had full confidence in our survivability. On October the 17th Jim and I did an unauthorized *Rhubarb* to France. I still recall the reprimand Jim received from [Flight Lieutenant Rhys] Thomas, the 'B' Flight commander …

"One of the barrage balloons in the area broke loose on October the 28th and was drifting across the Channel towards France. 'B' Flight was at readiness at the time and was detailed to shoot it down. Everyone wanted to go, so Thomas had us draw lots. Jim and I, [Sergeant Bryan] Waghorn and others. Waghorn won, but had engine failure and baled out over the Channel. We searched for him south of Worthing without success."[4]

On 1 November 1941, 129 Squadron was transferred to Debden for a rest and to re-train for night fighting sorties. After a number of personnel changes – departures, promotions, etc. – it returned to Westhampnett on 23

Left: Squadron Leader Dennis Armitage DFC was 129 (Mysore) Squadron's CO when it arrived at RAF Westhampnett. He was shot down on 21 September 1941, during a Wing escort for bombers on a *Circus* mission, and became a prisoner of war. A Battle of Britain pilot, Armitage was flying Spitfire Mk.Vb AD122 when he was shot down by Messerschmitt Bf 109s of *JG26*. Other squadron casualties that day were Sergeant Drew (rescued from the sea) and Sergeant C.L. MacDonald (killed in action). (Courtesy of Ray Sherk)

Right: Sergeant Ray Sherk, a Canadian who joined the RCAF in September 1940, was posted to 412 Squadron in early 1941 before joining 129 Squadron in July of that year. He claimed two victories whilst at Westhampnett. (Courtesy of Ray Sherk)

December. By this point, Thomas, now a squadron leader, had taken over as Commanding Officer, while Flight Lieutenant Henry Bowman had taken over as 'B' Flight commander.

Ray Sherk continues his account of life at Westhampnett, including 129 Squadron's participation in what came to be known as the Channel Dash, or Operation *Cerberus* to the Germans. In the course of this naval engagement, a *Kriegsmarine* force consisting of two battleships and the heavy cruiser *Prinz Eugen*, with escorts, ran a Royal Navy blockade and successfully sailed up the English Channel from Brest in Brittany to bases in Germany:

"One of the most memorable battles was the debacle on the 12th February when 129 Squadron distinguished itself. I was recalled from a sector reconnaissance due to the weather and the squadron was stood down. My diary entry reads, 'This a.m. led a formation with Hiskins and Bayliss for an hour. The weather was pretty bad when we came into land but we got in ok.

"We were called to readiness at noon (without dinner) and took off at 1.15 p.m. to escort some cannon-armed Hurricanes of No.1 Squadron to shoot-up some shipping off Calais that turned out to be the *Scharnhorst* and *Gneisenau* with some destroyers. Several aircraft missing.'

"[Pilot Officer] Dixie Davis was shot down and killed in action, [Flight Sergeant Hugh] MacPhee got a bullet in his shoe which grazed his heel and had several bullet holes in his aircraft. Sergeant Mick Wilson baled out over Ipswich after losing part of his starboard wing. Bowman got two 109s damaged.

"It was a pretty shaky do; I recall avoiding ship masts. I was involved in the melee but was not hit, although a shell from a destroyer just missed me. Upon our return, the intelligence officer, Flying Officer Chapman, was very interested in our individual recollections and we were interviewed extensively. It was much later on that we learned the full extent of the operation."[5]

The ORB for 129 Squadron records that twelve Spitfires were detailed for this mission, led by Squadron Leader Thomas:

"Squadron ordered to escort cannon Hurricanes of No 1 Squadron. After long delay of 1½ hours waiting at readiness, squadron took off as 6 Hurricanes circled Westhampnett and then flew to Hawkinge when rendezvous was made as arranged by Squadron Leader Thomas with Hurricane leader.

"After flying for 10 minutes out to sea 4 ships were seen and later 3 larger ones. The latter opened fire and the squadron covered the Hurricanes as they dived to attack. In the ensuing melee, P/O Davis said that his windscreen was oiled over and he was not seen again. Sgt Wilson was hit by flak but managed to get his machine back to England with half his starboard wing shot away, bailing [sic] out over Martlesham Heath.

Left: Sergeant Ray Sherk standing outside the sergeants' accommodation at Fishers Cottage. Located on the airfield's eastern boundary, close to the current entrance to Goodwood airfield and racetrack off Claypit Lane, Fishers Cottage was used throughout the war as pilots' accommodation. This picture appears to have been taken soon after 129 Squadron's arrival at Westhampnett, which was in August 1941. (Courtesy of Ray Sherk)

Opposite: A view of the east side of Fishers Cottage. The building can still be seen, though the thatched part in the background has long since gone. (Courtesy of Ray Sherk)

Flt/Sgt MacPhee was attacked by 3 Me 109s and was shot in the heel – his aircraft damaged but he returned safely to base. Flt/Lt Bowman attacked 2 Me 109s and damaged one and possibly another. Sgt Irish landed at West Malling short of petrol."[6]

Another of the RAF's squadrons involved in the Channel Dash was 41 Squadron which had recently been posted to Westhampnett. One of its pilots, Sergeant Robert Middlemiss, recalled his part in the events of 12 February 1942: "The squadron on this operation was led by S/L Hugo who destroyed one and damaged another enemy aircraft. P/O Roy Frank Cambridge destroyed a Bf 109 and F/S Ronald Edward Green destroyed one other of the enemy aircraft. Sgt Bruce Paul Dunstan was listed as missing on this operation."[7]

The next month, on 20 May, 129 Squadron was the subject of an official visit, as its ORB details: "Captain Binstead, the Trade Commissioner for Mysore, Mr. Goodchild of the India Office, and Sir Frank Brown of the East India Company, visited the Squadron, and after lunch with the Station Commander at Chopwyke [sic] House proceeded to the Dispersal where after speeches by Capt. Binstead and Sir Frank Brown, the latter presented Mysore Medallions to new pilots and to the ten Senior NCOs.

"This was followed by the arrival of the AOC, Air Vice Marshal Leigh Mallory, who presented the Squadron Crest (consisting of the Gundabherunda and the motto 'I Defend the Right') to the CO. After which the whole squadron marched past the AOC who took the salute and then received the pilots in the dispersal hut, congratulating them on the Squadron's record. Reference was made to the fact that 523 hours were

Opposite and Right: Sergeant Ray Sherk, of 129 Squadron, pictured in front of his Mk.Vb Spitfire at RAF Westhampnett. He nicknamed this aircraft *Shooting Star II*. (Courtesy of Ray Sherk)

flown by the squadron in February without a single accident."

Undoubtedly a cause for celebration, that evening a party was held at the communal site at Westerton. By this stage of the war, the airfield had outgrown its original boundaries and extended towards the local villages. A toast was drunk to the patron of the squadron, His Royal Highness the Maharajah of Mysore, who provided the funds for the party!

On 7 October 1941, the Tangmere Wing briefly included 65 (East India) Squadron, which was also based at Westhampnett, though it departed in December the same year, being replaced by 41 Squadron, the latter having moved the short distance from Merston. The new arrival's CO at this stage was Squadron Leader Petrus Hendrik 'Dutch' Hugo DFC and Bar, a South African who had fought with distinction in the Battle of Britain.

Sergeant (later Wing Commander) Bob Middlemiss recalls his time with 41 Squadron whilst at Westhampnett: "I was posted from 145 Squadron based at Catterick to 41 Squadron based at Merston on September 25th, 1941. The commanding officer was Squadron Leader 'Elmer' Gaunce, a Canadian who had joined the RAF in pre-war days.

"Merston was a grass field where we were able at times to take a whole squadron off in one go. The field was easy to find from the air because in one corner of the aerodrome were large hot-houses along with a very tall brick chimney. In bad weather they were the landmarks we looked for. As winter approached and the ground became too wet, we moved to Westhampnett … The adjutant of the squadron was Flying Officer Sherriff and the intelligence officer was Lord Guisborough. Flight Lieutenant Guisborough, who had been a pilot in the Royal Flying Corps in the First World War, had to suffer the pranks of enthusiastic young Spitfire pilots. In debriefings they would pull silly things, exaggerating what they had seen on the mission, or saying things like – 'Shot down a battleship today'.

"The groundcrew were led by Flight Sergeant 'Tiny' Thompson. My Spitfire coded 'EB-J' *Hazel* was looked after by Joe Parfitt, my rigger, and Wally Chapman, my fitter, both great guys. Two other groundcrew we saw and dealt with a lot were LAC Muller and LAC Wootton. They operated the telephones at the squadron dispersal and were the ones who received the calls from 'ops centre' to 'scramble' after an approaching raid.

"We were billeted at 'Woodcote Farm' a lovely old house with beautiful and well cared-for lawns. It was a very pleasant area to rest when off duty … The pubs we enjoyed [in Chichester] were the 'Rose & Crown' and the 'Unicorn'. Many 'mild and bitter' pints were consumed while enjoying the good humour of endless Air Force songs and ditties as well as games of darts and shuffleboard. There was also a movie theatre in the town as well as a lovely café where dances were regularly held … The great friendliness of the local people was remarkable."[8]

The departure of 41 Squadron led to the arrival of the Free French at Westhampnett, more specially 340 (Île-de-France) Squadron.[9] The Frenchmen flew alongside 129 Squadron from April to July, when the latter departed to make way for the USAAF.

Most of the operations that were undertaken during the early months of 1942 were sweeps or bomber escorts over northern France, raids which were mostly led by the Wing Leader at the time, Wing Commander H. de C.A. 'Paddy' Woodhouse.

Another important date in the history of Westhampnett came on 30 May 1942, when a detachment of Hawker Typhoons from 56 (Punjab) Squadron flew in from Duxford under the command of Squadron Leader H. 'Cocky' Dundas. Dundas was no stranger to the airfield having flown with 616 Squadron throughout the summer of 1941. The extra noise that the Typhoons' Napier Sabre engines created was recalled by a local resident, a telephone engineer by the name of Jenks: "Yes, they made a terrible noise; there was a crowd of them that came over Goodwood and roared. It was deafening. I remember seeing them at Apuldram – the 'Happydrome' they

Above: One of 129 Squadron's Spitfire Mk.Vs, in this case AA754 which was coded 'DV-L', parked on Westhampnett's eastern boundary. This is the view looking north towards some of the cottages used for accommodation. As AA754 had its first flight with the squadron on 3 October 1941, it is likely that this image was taken in early 1942. (Courtesy of Ray Sherk)

used to call it. When a squadron came into land it was deafening. You can't have the locals being upset by that sort of thing."[10]

There were further problems for the Typhoons, such as on 5 June when one of the 56 Squadron pilots taxied into one of 129 Squadron's Spitfires, leaving the latter a virtual write-off. Such incidents aside, whilst at Westhampnett the Typhoons mostly undertook patrols along the South Coast in conjunction with a second flight from 56 Squadron which was based at RAF Manston.

Though it only remained at Westhampnett until 7 June 1942, 56 Squadron's time there features in a surviving section of film footage from Pathé News. In this, Dundas can be seen taking off towards the south-west in Typhoon US-'A'. Identifiable features in the footage are the water tower at Graylingwell whilst the spire of Chichester Cathedral can clearly be seen as Dundas passes the perimeter track.

The squadron's officers were mostly accommodated at both Woodcote and at Shopwyke House where they attended social gatherings and dances. Alternatively, the pilots would often all go down to Pagham to the King's Beach Hotel to dine. When off duty the pilots would sometimes head to Pagham Harbour to bathe and relax.

Danger, though, was never very far away. On 19 June, for example, patrols were sent up from Westhampnett during dusk readiness. Whilst in the air, 129 Squadron's Blue Section was jumped by two Focke-Wulf Fw 190s hiding in the thick haze. Sergeant B.R. McCormack was killed when his Spitfire Vb (BL244) was shot down near Sidlesham. Sergeant E. Irish chased both of the enemy raiders but was unable to make any claim; he was slightly wounded in the leg and his aircraft was hit in several places.[11]

Though 129 Squadron was coming to the end of its time at Westhampnett, one incident on 1 July 1942 highlights the dangers of operational flying under wartime conditions. One patrol that day involved Sergeant R.L. Reeves as Red 1, with Sergeant M.W. Firth as his No.2. They had both been warned by control that there were bandits in their area. The

squadron's ORB includes this description of what happened next: "After several vectors, control warned Red 1 of bandits in the immediate vicinity and at the same time Red 2 warned him of an aircraft on his tail. He broke sharply and fired at aircraft diving on him from the sun. As the latter turned over and burst into flames it was seen to be a Spitfire. The No.2 of the other aircraft continued to behave in a hostile manner to Red 2 till the latter turned and faced him."[12]

The pilots in the other two aircraft were Squadron Leader Bobby Oxspring DFC of 72 Squadron and Group Captain Barwell DFC, who was the Commanding Officer of RAF Biggin Hill. Both men were undertaking a standing patrol; the pair had also been warned of unidentified aircraft in their area. The ORB of 72 Squadron, for the following day, states: "The squadron learnt today [2 July] that Group Captain Barwell, DFC, the station commander at Biggin Hill, was shot down when on patrol with S/Ldr R.W. Oxspring DFC 15 miles south-west of Beachy Head. They had taken off together from Biggin Hill in the late evening with a view to intercepting the Hun reconnaissance aircraft that for the past fortnight has flown over the south-east coast at 21.00 hours, and owing to a tragic mistake, G/Capt Barwell was fired on by one of two other Spitfires of 129 Squadron (Tangmere) on patrol, and shot down in flames. He did not bale out."[13]

This account lays the blame for this 'friendly-fire' incident at the feet of the 129 Squadron pilots. In his book *Spitfire Command* Oxspring wrote: "A subsequent enquiry revealed that of the two pilots, one was on his first operational flight, the other on his second … neither being competent

---

Right: Pilot Officer James Henry Whalen (on the left) being congratulated after his third 'kill', a Messerschmitt Bf 109E on 21 September 1941, at RAF Westhampnett. His previous two 'kills' were both Bf 109s. (Courtesy of Ray Sherk)

enough to recognise a Spitfire even at closest possible quarters."[14] For its part, the 129 Squadron ORB concludes that, "this very regrettable accident was in no way attributable to the pilots but was due to confusion arising from 2 sections from different Sectors being vectored on to the same interception without liaison between Controls".[15]

Prior to this disaster, at the end of June 1942 another squadron arrived at Westhampnett in the form of 416 (City of Oshawa) Squadron, an RCAF unit with which 129 Squadron carried out Wing practice flights. Then, in July, two United States Army Air Force (USAAF) pilots, supported by four mechanics, arrived on attachment to 129 Squadron to gain operational experience. Amongst this small group was Captain Harrison Thyng, who was shortly to command the first squadron of Americans posted to Westhampnett, the 309th Fighter Squadron, in August 1942. He took part in his first operation on 19 July. By the end of the month, however, 129 Squadron had been posted out to Thorney Island.

The Americans who replaced 129 Squadron at Westhampnett were some of the first pilots of the 31st Fighter Group to see combat in the European Theatre. With their arrival, RAF Westhampnett also became the USAAF's base No.352.[16] The 31st Fighter Group had deployed to the UK in June 1942. It comprised three squadrons – the 307th, 308th and 309th Fighter Squadrons – all of which were equipped with Spitfire Mk.Vs. It was the 309th that was sent to Westhampnett.[17]

The 31st Fighter Group was declared operational at the start of August 1942, beginning combat operations on the 2nd – for the 309th, more specifically, this was slightly later on 9 August. Serving with the latter, Lieutenant Harry Strawn maintained a meticulous diary. Along with his letters home, it paints a vivid picture of Westhampnett during this period.

Of his arrival at Westhampnett on 4 August, Strawn wrote: "The weather finally broke this morning and at last we had chance to get off to Westhampnett. 'A' Flight took off first and about half an hour latter 'B'

Flight got under way. The journey was very fast, actually, and before I realized it we were on the English Channel and our new base.

"The field is very well camouflaged and at first I didn't see it. It's a grass field, but very nice indeed. Our Quarters are a bit different now, as I'm living in an old mansion. Spike Schofield and I have a room on the second floor. We are not far from the field now. In fact I can look out of my window and see my 'plane from here. It's a change to be in something like a home, even if it's old."

The pilots of the 309th's 'A' Flight were accommodated in Woodcote Farm, whilst those of 'B Flight, Strawn included, found themselves in Fishers Cottage, the partly-thatched farm house on the boundary of the airfield. That the Americans were now on the front line was evidenced by his diary entry the following day:

"Got up this morning to the sound of the siren which tells me that Jerry is around somewhere, but it didn't seem to bother me at all; in fact, I rather enjoyed it. For most of the morning we were at lectures receiving instructions from the British – and its all good stuff. Lectures on radio silence, tactical formation, security of information, how to get in your dinghy if you had to bail [sic] out in the channel etc. I spent a good bit of time with Sgt Hariss with my new Spit, telling him what I wanted done to my plane. My number is 'WZ-X' and as yet I haven't decided on a name

Right: Pilot Officer James Henry Whalen in the cockpit of his 129 Squadron Spitfire Mk.Vb, W8707 (coded 'DV-R'), at RAF Westhampnett during September 1941. In fact this picture was taken on the airfield's northern boundary. Note that all three of Whalen's 'kills' are marked on the side of the cockpit, as is the family crest. Whalen was later posted to the Far East, being shot down and killed on 18 April 1944, when he was leading a flight of 34 Squadron Hurricanes on a raid to Kohima. He is buried in Kohima War Cemetery. (Courtesy of Ray Sherk)

for my plane. I flew it for two hours today, first to get familiar with the countryside and also to see what I could get out of my plane."

On 8 August, Strawn noted that the 309th "became semi-operational, i.e. we are now taking an active part in this strange war". It was also the day on which the squadron had its first encounter with the *Luftwaffe*. A few of the 309th's Spitfires were airborne on gunnery practice over Shoreham-by-Sea when they were directed to intercept a plot by controllers. At this point in the war the Germans were directing tip-and-run raiders, often bomb-carrying Fw 190s, to hit targets on the South Coast. These raiders would come in low and fast, drop their lethal load and turn for home. Strawn described what happened:

"We were all rather excited and everyone was anxious to get 'cracking', however the weather was very bad and as a result the day was fairly quiet. I spent the biggest part of the day waxing 'Beverly' – that's my Spit which has now been christened – and getting her in shape for the big show … Some of the boys did go off on a scramble this evening and [the recently promoted] Major Thyng ran in to two Fw 190s. However, he only damaged one, at least that's his story, which won't be credited to him. We were on alert until 10.30pm and during this time we had five air raid alarms but saw nothing."

One of Strawn's first hair-raising moments as a fighter pilot occurred on Tuesday, 11 August: "At one o'clock we went on alert and I was to fly with Salty Chambers in Blue Section which was first off. We got a scramble but I had a hell of a time getting *Bev* started and then when I did get off we came back in and landed for Jerry must have turned back. I had a close call after landing, for another plane came in and hit so hard he had to go off again and he almost hit me. It turned out to be Colonel Hawkins – the big dog."[18]

A defining moment for the American Spitfire pilots came on 17 August: "At 3:15pm we all went to the briefing hut [on the eastern boundary near the current entrance, where four huts had been erected] to get the 'gen' on a sweep we were to participate in. It was a big sweep using some 360 Spitfires and 18 American Flying Fortresses. We were to act as rear cover for the bombers and had to pick them up on their way out from France. Every bomber got back safely and also all the Spits. There were plenty of Jerries but they didn't want to fight. I didn't go myself but I watched the show from the operational room and it really is something to see."

This rear cover operation, part of *Circus* 204, was led by Major McNickle of the 307th, who took off with twelve Spitfires, accompanied by Wing Commander Thomas, at 17.15 hours. The fighters flew in to trouble at 27,000 feet over the French coast and both McNickle and Thomas fired long bursts at Fw 190s, though with no visible success. All of the Spitfires returned safely. This was the first occasion on which the US pilots had experienced aerial combat. There was, however, much more to come – and sooner than expected.

"We had a secret meeting and got some real 'gen'," noted Strawn in his diary on 18 August. "Tomorrow we have a big show starting at four a.m. Some 31 fighter squadrons, 2,000 Canadian soldiers, Commandos, bombers and boats are going to make landings at the town of Dieppe on the coast of France. We are going to destroy the entire town and hold it for one day. Our job is to escort the boats across the Channel. Of course we will be fighting Fw 190s all day. It should be a big show and my first fight. I'll need strength tomorrow."

Despite the scale of the events surrounding the Dieppe Raid, Strawn's diary of 19 August was perhaps not as detailed as it could have been: "I

Right: Pilot Officer Victor Tucker being helped by groundcrew to climb into his 129 Squadron Spitfire at RAF Westhampnett, prior to participating in a sweep over northern France. Tucker, a Jamaican who had qualified as a barrister before the war, joined up in August 1940 and was posted to 129 Squadron in 1941. (Courtesy of Ray Sherk)

guess this is the big day of my life for I got a real taste of aerial warfare. I got up at 3am this morning and by the time we got to the field everyone was really busy. Planes warming up in the dark and others in the air on their way to Dieppe, France, for the big day. Most of us were joking and laughing, but I rather imagine it was to cover up there nerves. I know I felt a bit on edge and a little shaky.

"Our first mission was at 9.00am in the morning and the boys really ran in to hell in the skies. When they came back, two of our planes were missing. Collins baled out about five miles from the French coast after getting his engine shot up by an Fw 190; Junkin got a 20mm shell in his shoulder and baled out. Both were picked up by boat. My mission turned out very good as we were not attacked by anything. However, the ground flak was terrific but it didn't bother me much."

In due course, Strawn elaborated further: "I guess you read about the Battle of Dieppe and there isn't much I could add except for our own bird's eye viewpoint. I rather imagine the papers gave a very full account of it, for they questioned us for a solid three hours and believe me, newspaper men are inquisitive. Even *Life*'s famous woman photographer [Margaret B. White] was here to take pictures and I don't know how many newsreel men.

"However, I might say it was a big day for us, for we came out very well. We lost only three planes and all of the pilots got out safely. One of our boys got the first German Fw 190 but, in doing so, was shot down by

---

Left: A picture of 129 Squadron's Pilot Officer Victor Emmanuel Tucker in his flying kit at RAF Westhampnett just before a sortie. He was shot up and his Spitfire badly damaged during *Circus* 122 to Hazebrouck marshalling yards on 12 April 1942, though he returned safely. Tucker was shot down and killed on a *Rodeo* to Le Havre on 4 May 1942. (Courtesy of Ray Sherk)

Right: Left to right are Flying Officer Hugo Throssell Armstrong, Flight Lieutenant Rhys Thomas and Pilot Officer James Henry 'Jimmy' Whalen, all pilots with 129 Squadron, at RAF Westhampnett in September 1941. An Australian, Armstrong was credited with three confirmed kills whilst flying with 129 Squadron. He went on to achieve twelve confirmed kills, and be awarded the DFC and Bar, before being shot down and killed whilst leading 611 (West Lancashire) Squadron on 5 February 1943. Armstrong was named after his uncle, Hugo Throssell, who was awarded the Victoria Cross for his actions at Gallipoli in the First World War. Thomas was a Battle of Britain veteran, having flown with Nos. 64, 66 and 266 squadrons. He later became the Commanding Officer of 129 Squadron on 2 January 1942, eventually becoming the Wing Leader at RAF Tangmere in July 1943. Thomas was also awarded a DFC and DSO. (Courtesy of Ray Sherk)

another Fw 190. However he is getting along ok and what is more he will get the DFC and the Purple Heart. We are very proud of him and naturally so.

"As for myself, you might say I was born under a lucky star, at least I believe I was. With things as hot as they were, I can't understand how I got out, but I did. The Germans are plenty good, and have a good fighter plane in the Fw 190, but I believe we are better. Of course it doesn't pay to get 'cocky' for about that time you'll wake up to find that you've had it. You have to keep your eyes open all the time and looking around, for in most cases they come down on you from above and out of the sun … We have a good plane to meet them within the Spitfire, and one the British should be very proud off. For myself I hope I never have to fly any other make in this man's war."

Whilst Dieppe had been the first real test for the Americans, there was no time to rest. Indeed, on the 20th Strawn participated in *Circus* 207, another sweep over France. That evening, it was the enemy's >> (Page 116)

Left: Sergeant Raymond Wilson also participated in the Channel Dash operations, when a third of the wing of his Spitfire (W3800) was shot away by anti-aircraft fire, forcing him to bale out. In his collection, the author has Wilson's Irvin parachute bag, C-Type flying helmet and gold Caterpillar Club badge. (Author's Collection)

Opposite: Another picture of 129 (Mysore) Squadron personnel in front of the Duty Pilot hut on the western boundary of the airfield at Westhampnett. From left to right, are: Drew, Sangerhaus, Davis, Manly, Wilson and Dalton. Sergeant Henry William Sangerhaus was killed in action on 13 February 1942, whilst operating from Westhampnett. Pilot Officer George Davis RCAF lost his life during the Channel Dash on 12 February 1942, whilst flying Spitfire Mk.Vb AA921. (Courtesy of Ray Sherk)

Opposite page: Pilots of 129 Squadron at RAF Westhampnett towards the end of September 1941. In the back row, from left to right, are: Flying Officer Walker (Medical Officer), Sergeant Wilson, Sergeant Bryan Waghorn (shot down and killed on 28 October 1941), Sergeant McPhee (killed in action), Flight Lieutenant Henry Bowman DFC (killed in action, 28 July 1942), Pilot Officer Gordon Walker (missing in action, 13 October 1941), Pilot Officer James Whalen (killed in action, 1944), Pilot Officer G. Davis (killed on the Channel Dash operation), Pilot Officer Cunliffe, Pilot Officer Hugo Armstrong (killed in action, 5 February 1943), Pilot Officer Vic Tucker (killed in action), Sergeant Sergeant, Sergeant Ray Sherk, Sergeant Ramsay (killed in action whilst serving on Malta), Sergeant Hardy, Flying Officer Davis (Administration) and Flying Officer Wally Chapman (Intelligence Officer). In the front row, again left to right, are: Flight Lieutenant R. Thomas, Squadron Leader Abrahams (CO), Group Captain 'Woody' Woodhall, un-named Administration Officer and Flight Lieutenant McPherson (shot down and captured, 13 October 1941). (Courtesy of Ray Sherk)

Above: A photograph of all of 129 Squadron's personnel, including groundcrew, also taken towards the end of September 1941. (Courtesy of Ray Sherk)

Above: One of 129 Squadron's Spitfires, in this case Mk.Vb 'DV-L', pictured after it came to grief during a ground loop. The pilot on this occasion was Pilot Officer Gordon Walker. The picture was taken looking towards Westhampnett's eastern boundary. (Courtesy of Ray Sherk)

Right: Flying Officer Edward Chapman, the Intelligence Officer for 129 Squadron, pictured in the snow at RAF Westhampnett during the winter of 1941/1942. Chapman was also a well-known actor and starred in nearly 100 films, most notably as Mr Grimsdale in the Norman Wisdom films. (Courtesy of Ray Sherk)

Below: Two members of 41 Squadron's groundcrew, rigger Joe Parfitt (on the left) and fitter Wally Chapman (on the right), beside Bob Middlemiss' Spitfire Vb, which was nicknamed *Hazel*. (Courtesy of the late Wing Commander Robert George 'Bob' Middlemiss, DFC, CD)

Left: Pilot Officer Victor Emmanuel Tucker and another pilot, identified only as Sims, pictured in front of a 129 Squadron Spitfire, a photograph believed to have been taken at Westhampnett in 1941. (Courtesy of Ray Sherk)

turn to go on the attack. "I had a hard time sleeping last night for the Jerries bombed Portsmouth for about an hour," commented Strawn in his diary on the 21st, "and we could hear it in Chichester. In fact our house was shaking from the blasts as a result."

As August drew to a close, the 309th was joined in Sussex by the remainder of the 31st Fighter Group, the 307th moving to Merston and the 308th to Westhampnett. No doubt it was partly due to the fact that the three squadrons had been concentrated together that, on 27 August, the US pilots had their "pictures taken by about 100 cameramen and newspaper men" – as mentioned previously, the Dieppe Raid featured heavily. It would appear, however, that things had been said on this occasion that displeased the authorities – as Strawn noted on 3 September:

"We received word from General Frank today that in the future we will not express our opinions on British Spitfires. In other words he gave us Hell for telling the 'press' the truth. Yes, we are not to say that the Spit is the best fighter plane in the world. He wants us to keep the people back home from knowing the truth.

"As yet the US has no fighter plane that can touch anything the British Spit can, much less the Me 109F or the Fw 190. We as pilots know what a good plane is, but the people at home will never know that the P40 and the P39 would be death traps in this war. I hope to God that we will never get them here for we wouldn't have a chance against the Germans. That's the kind of man that leads us.

"When they get the money-making politicians out of power then perhaps we will build a good plane. I wish someone would drop a bomb on the Allison plant and the Bell plant; it may save a lot of American boys their lives."

In mid-September, the 31st Fighter Group was ordered to pack and crate its equipment and stores for a long-distance move. Rumours of a transfer to Egypt or North Africa were rife. When the eventual transfer began, on 9 October 1942, it was indeed to North Africa.

For the first time in its history, Westhampnett became the base for a twin-engine fighter when Lockheed P-38 Lightnings of the 48th and 49th Fighter Squadrons, part of the 14th Fighter Group, arrived to gain operational experience on 1 October. Some fourteen P-38s flew from Westhampnett before departing a couple of weeks later on the 15th.

The next squadron to move in was already familiar with RAF Westhampnett, having been stationed there in 1941. This was 616 (South Yorkshire) Squadron, now flying the Spitfire Mk.VI.

The squadron was led by Squadron Leader Harry Lennox Innes Brown DFC, a veteran pilot who had flown Gloster Gladiators against the Italians with 112 Squadron. This squadron remained until 2 January 1943.

Another unit in residence around the same time was 124 (Baroda) Squadron, also equipped with the high-altitude Spitfire Mk.VI. This squadron did not stay long, its place taken by 131 (County of Kent) Squadron flying the Spitfire Mk.V.

Right: Sergeant Tony Drew, 129 Squadron, pictured in front of one of the tin-roofed blister hangars erected on the airfield for maintenance. Drew was shot down on 21 September 1941, whilst providing escort to a force of bombers attacking Gosnay power station, large numbers of Bf 109s being engaged over Le Touquet. He was rescued from the sea by an RAF air sea rescue launch. (Courtesy of Ray Sherk)

By this stage of the war RAF Westhampnett had already been home to airmen of many nationalities, including those from the UK, United States, France, Norway, Canada, Belgium, Poland, Australia, South Africa and even Jamaica. The next country to lay claim to the airfield was New Zealand, the pilots and groundcrew of 485 (NZ) Squadron arriving on 1 January 1943.

Formed at Driffield in Yorkshire in 1941, the squadron's groundcrew were initially all RAF personnel. Leading Aircraftman Joe Roddis was amongst the latter who joined the squadron on its formation: "I was put on 'A' Flight and allocated aircraft 'OU-F'. The rigger on the plane responsible for airframe servicing was Danny McWhinnie from Musselborough near Edinburgh, and I was the engine man … The outstanding difference the groundcrew noticed, and often commented on, was the much more sociable and relaxed atmosphere that existed between the New Zealand aircrew and us groundcrew. We were made to feel part of the team and not just an 'erk'."[19]

Under the command of Squadron Leader Reginald Grant DFC, DFM the squadron was posted to RAF Westhampnett on 1 January 1943. Roddis recalls the accommodation that the airmen were billeted in: "We headed south … to this satellite of RAF Tangmere in January 1943 and the

Opposite: A group of 129 Squadron pilots and personnel pictured in the snow at RAF Westhampnett, probably in the early weeks of January 1942. From left to right, they are: Hiskins, Sergeant, Davis, Hardy, Cunliffe, Thomas, Bush, Armstrong and 'Wally' Chapman, the Intelligence Officer. (Courtesy of Ray Sherk)

Right: Sergeant Ray Sherk in his flying gear at Westhampnett in the winter of 1941/1942. He is wearing a first pattern C-Type leather flying helmet with rubber ear cups, rather than the earlier B-Type with the leather ear cups, with Mk.IVa flying goggles. In November 1941, Ray was recommended for promotion to Pilot Officer. (Courtesy of Ray Sherk)

squadron was quickly operational within hours of arriving. We lived in huts a fair distance from the dispersal, but all facilities and food were good and plenty to do in Chichester any time we got off."

It was a busy time on the airfield – Roddis recalls that for the groundcrew the days were often long: "Early morning readiness meant being by your aircraft by 3a.m. and we'd stand down at the end of the day when all aircraft were serviceable, ready for the next day's operations. This could often be around midnight."[20]

One of 485 Squadron's pilots was Flying Officer Doug Brown: "[Our] officers were accommodated in a two storied house called Fishers Cottage on the aerodrome perimeter. The mess for meals was a Nissen hut about 100 metres from our accommodation. This was only used for meals as we established a lounge and bar at Fishers Cottage. The Sergeants' accommodation was Nissen huts at this time.

"As with most squadrons we 'worked and played hard'. The Mermaid Hotel, about halfway from the aerodrome to Chichester, was well patronised by 485. … The proprietor was a very generous host, not only to 485 but all RAF squadrons. The squadron also utilised the services of the King's Beach Hotel at Pagham. In the main we entertained our 'friends' at Fishers Cottage. The squadron was fully involved in flying duties and more often than not pilots were involved in two or more operations a day".[21]

Above: Three Norwegian replacement pilots for 129 (Mysore) Squadron pictured after their arrival at a snow-covered RAF Westhampnett in the early weeks of 1942. From left to right they are: Gronmark, Strand (wearing what appears to be an American flying jacket) and Ulstein (in an Irvin flying jacket). Though it is not clear to see, Gronmark is holding Smoky, a small dog that served as a squadron mascot. The Duty Pilot hut in the background was located on the western boundary of the airfield. (Courtesy of Ray Sherk)

Opposite: Flight Lieutenant Rhys Henry Thomas, 129 Squadron's 'B' Flight commander, having just landed at RAF Westhampnett. A Battle of Britain veteran, Thomas claimed a Focke-Wulf Fw 190 destroyed on 5 May 1942, and damaged another on 17 August 1942. Following the shooting down and capture of Squadron Leader Dennis Armitage DFC, Thomas was eventually, in January 1942, given command of the squadron. He later the Tangmere Wing leader. (Courtesy of Ray Sherk)

In a letter home to his family in January 1943, Brown expanded on his squadron's role at the time, picking on one particular sortie: "We did a rather good *Circus* to Abbeville. We went over as independent wings while two bombing raids were undertaken on two 'dromes to try and get the Huns up. The Fortresses went farther in. We got the Huns up ok but did not get a bounce. One of the other wings got a few. It was good to be at least close enough to mark the good old black crosses. I was watching the Jerry come down, but I could not get into a position to get a shot."

With the *Luftwaffe* was still carrying out its low-level tip-and-run raids, the Tangmere Wing had a constant patrol operating from dawn to dusk. There were other duties, as Brown explained: "I was deputy Flight Commander when, on dawn readiness [on] 11 April 1943, my number 2 and I were scrambled to cover the return of a damaged Stirling bomber. We located the aircraft, which was forced to make a landing in the sea a mile or so off Shoreham. All the crew except one had managed to clamber into the rubber dinghy.

"One crew member in his Mae West was drifting out to sea and I considered I could drop him my dinghy. I dropped the speed to 120mph, put down my flaps and with much difficulty managed to remove the dinghy from my parachute pack, which I was sitting on. I released the dinghy but forgot it had a lead attached and it caught the rudder area. Fortunately the air pressure broke the cord as I had almost stalled due to the low speed. Regretfully it did not hit the target … but a Walrus was soon on the scene and made the rescue.

On 20 January 1943, 610 (County of Chester) Squadron returned to Westhampnett under the command of Squadron Leader Johnnie Johnson who had been with 616 Squadron at the airfield back in 1941.

One of the characters from 610 Squadron to grace the airfield during this period was Flying Officer Colin Hodgkinson. Hodgkinson had lost both of his legs above the knee whilst training with the Fleet Air Arm.

Undeterred, he re-applied for the RAF and was accepted on the basis that Douglas Bader had been cleared to fly before him.

Hodgkinson was duly posted to 610 Squadron at Westhampnett. The airfield therefore gained the distinction of seeing both of the RAF's legless pilots stationed there during the war. Hodgkinson recalled the type of operations that he and his colleagues were involved with: "The Wing was taking a box of Mitchells briefed to bomb Poix Aerodrome near Amiens. Things were quiet on the way over. I was feeling confident, glued to my No.1 with engine singing sweetly and the entire Wing reassuringly visible in the clear air … We crossed the coast, flew on in silence and then, as the Mitchells queued up for their run, the controllers voice came in: 'Forty plus bandits climbing to meet you from the south-west'."

The opposing forces clashed and Hodgkinson soon lost his No.1 in the ensuing melee. He could see aircraft going down in smoke and parachutes opening – but no enemy aircraft. Isolated and alone, he turned tightly and noticed four Fw 190s diving down on him. They fired and missed; he survived to fight another day.

That night the pilots went into Chichester for a few drinks at The Unicorn pub, a favourite haunt of theirs which was run by Arthur King. After closing hours it was decided that the party should continue back at Westhampnett, as Hodgkinson recalled: "When we got back some three hours later to Woodcote Farm – the house on the edge of the aerodrome where we had our quarters – there seemed no good reason why the party should die. There was drink, mainly beer, but the fire in the hall was out and the night very cold. We were not in a state to let this be an excuse for going to bed. The coal cellar being either shut or empty – I can't recall which – we set about groping around for wood. But the only wood in sight was the bannisters up the wide stone steps which led to the floor above. They were old and looked temptingly inflammable. Within five minutes they were torn out, broken up and providing a splendid blaze. Round this we sat for another hour, drinking mulled beer and singing ribald songs."

Above: A group of pilots from 129 Squadron relax in the sun outside the dispersal at RAF Westhampnett. The original caption states "Spring at last", this referring to the early months of 1942. From left to right, they are: Loree, Govert Steen, 'Freddie', Ramsay, Cole, Manly and Jan, the squadron's dog. Govert Steen was an interesting character, having managed to steal a Fokker T.VIIw from the Germans and escape to the UK on the night of 5/6 May 1941. He flew a total of seventy-nine sorties before being shot down and killed, on 5 June 1942, whilst flying from Westhampnett. (Courtesy of Ray Sherk)

Left: The billets and mess used by 129 (Mysore) Squadron at RAF Westhampnett. It is thought that the location was on the airfield's western boundary. None of these buildings survive today, though the dispersal and some concrete bases can be identified from the air. (Courtesy of Ray Sherk)

At about 03.00 hours in the morning, Hodgkinson suddenly remembered that he was on operations – an attack on Brest – in a few hours' time. In fact the briefing was at 08.30 hours.

"I heaved myself up, gave an expansive good night to my friends and rolled towards the stairs," he continued. "But Arthur's rum and the heady stench of burning varnish had had their effect. At that stage of my progress in walking I could get up stairs without using bannisters, although I preferred them to be there. There was no doubt that I needed them now. All went well until I had got nearly to the top when, losing my balance, I slow-rolled sideways and outwards, clutched wildly at where the bannisters should have been and fell like a log some nine feet to the floor beneath. I landed on my head and the fall knocked me out completely."[22]

Put to bed by his colleagues, Hodgkinson was woken by Johnnie Johnson shaking him and asking him if he was fit to fly. The state of Hodgkinson's face suggested otherwise, and he was duly replaced on that morning's operation.

The New Zealand squadron moved out of Westhampnett at the end of June. Prior to its departure a steady stream of newcomers moved in, including 167 and 501 (County of Gloucester) squadrons, both still equipped with Spitfire Mk.Vs. Then on 19 June the Spitfire Mk.XII-equipped 41 Squadron flew in from RAF Friston – these were some of the first Spitfires to be fitted with the Rolls-Royce Griffon engine. That same month 91 (Nigeria) Squadron also arrived flying the same aircraft.

The pilots were accommodated at both Fishers Cottage and Shopwyke House. Many of the groundcrew were billeted at Westerton, which at that time had been considerably developed. No.41 Squadron's time at Westhampnett is described by one of its pilots, Pilot Officer Peter Graham: "On the 21st June [sic] we moved to Westhampnett, a satellite of Tangmere, which was one of our busiest fighter stations. The move signalled the end of that cautious period when we were forbidden to risk getting shot down over enemy territory … It was now time for us to go on the offensive.

"We were an odd bunch. My flight commander was Doug Hone. He was warm hearted and an excellent leader but he didn't stay with us for long. I think he was probably given his own squadron but all I know for sure is he left us in June 41 to be replaced by 'Pinky' Glenn, who was probably the most inspiring of the various officers under whom I served and who latter was to come back and command the squadron.

"Other notable characters were Tom Slack, then a Flying Officer, later to be my flight commander. He was a cartoonist of great talent. Two other NCO pilots, with whom I resumed contacts many years later, were Jim Payne and Peter Wall, and Joe Birbeck, about my age but a Flying Officer at the time and more often than not my number one.

"We never flew operationally except in pairs or greater numbers. This was to ensure that we could defend each other and keep sharp lookout in all directions. At this time the principal operation was the sweep, which involved the squadron flying as a unit as escort to or a distraction from the bomber force attacking targets in northern France or shipping around the ports. Sometimes we simply went looking for trouble hoping to spot enemy aircraft.

"By far the most exciting kind of operation, I felt, was the *Rhubarb*. Now and again the odd pilot who had achieved number one status would get permission to take his number two on a low level recco over northern France just seeking out likely targets.

"It was on one of these excursions [that] I got in to my first, and arguably my worst, bit of trouble. Joe Birbeck and I had ranged around for about twenty minutes over France and had hit nothing more important than a defenceless water tower. It was time to go home; so we headed north – leaving France close to St Valery, hedge hopping. The theory was no anti-aircraft gunner would be able to react swiftly enough to hit us.

"On this occasion it didn't turn out that way. As we crossed the coast there was an almighty bang and everything changed. After the roar and racket of the past quarter of an hour there was suddenly silence. There was glass everywhere except in the instrument panel where it belonged. My right arm would not obey my commands but hung loose at my side. Almost every dial, indicator and gauge in front of me had gone haywire. I was stone deaf!

"I had received a direct hit from a forty millimetre anti-aircraft shell that exploded on the armour plate behind my head. Two or three inches further forward and it would have blown my head off. I was flying fairly comfortably just keeping formation with my number one until we got back to Westhampnett.

"He landed first and I circled the airfield and could see no sign of a crash wagon or ambulance. I was a bit bothered by this as I didn't know if I'd get the undercarriage down or whether I'd know if it was down and locked. I didn't fancy doing a wheels-up landing but probably I should have seriously considered it or alternatively flown across to Tangmere to make my touch down at a really big station with all the facilities.

"I've sometimes wondered why, when I was severely handicapped and my Spitfire in dire shape, I chose to land at Westhampnett rather than at Tangmere where on the face of it I would have been much safer. The answer, I think, is that Westhampnett was 'home' in a way that Tangmere was not.

"In the end I flew over the airfield a couple of times, waggling my wings. Then I climbed to three thousand feet in order to execute the quite difficult manoeuvre of lowering the undercarriage with my left hand. It was now that I greatly appreciated that I had a functioning air speed indicator. I could cross the hedge just above stalling speed and touch down

as planned. In fact the landing seemed so good that I didn't cut the engine. My Spit behaved superbly, stopping just short of the further hedge.

"I turned and taxied towards our dispersal. I glanced down at my right arm and received a shock. Blood was welling out over the top of my flying gauntlet. At the same moment someone was getting the canopy off and I yelled 'get the blood wagon' and promptly fainted.

"The next thing I knew I was in the back of an ambulance with our MO [medical officer], Doc. Burnett, sitting beside me, just having completed [applying] a tourniquet to my damaged arm. I soon found myself tucked up in bed in St Richard's hospital.

"When the surgeon visited me to tell me all had gone well, he handed me a lump of metal, which I have carefully preserved as a souvenir, and told me this was by far the biggest bit he'd got out of me. I had seventeen days in hospital and then a fortnight's sick leave.

"I was back in the air on the 25th August, getting used to flying again and doing a bit of practice on ground targets with my cine-gun. Two days later I was flying with the whole squadron on a sweep escorting B17s. We had quite a dodgy time and from our point of view a sad one. The Forts carried out their mission but we lost two pilots, one of whom baled out; the other was missing. We'd spent a lot of time at full throttle and were therefore low on fuel by the time the action was over. We flew to Ford, which was our nearest RAF station.

"We celebrated the fourth anniversary of the outbreak of war with a sweep, giving close escort to thirty-six Marauders. The next day a similar mission, but this time Joe Birbeck and I were lucky enough to be able to

Opposite: Sergeant Ray Sherk (centre) with two of his groundcrew at RAF Westhampnett; to his right is Hopwell, to his left is Faulds. Note Ray's parachute resting on the wing of his Spitfire Mk.V, which is at readiness at dispersal. (Courtesy of Ray Sherk)

engage a pair of Fw 190s that were attacking some Spitfire Vs below us. He shot one down and almost at the same moment I was hit. I thought by flak.

"My engine temperature gauge began to climb so I headed straight for home, or rather for Ford, where I landed without trouble. As I suspected there was a hole in the radiator, which I put down to flak but latter learnt that in fact the damage was caused by bullet clips, presumably emanating from the guns of my number one …

"The 26th September was celebrated as Battle of Britain Day. 41 Squadron played its part by buzzing the City of Chichester in close formation and generally displaying our aerobatic skills at low altitude. Nowadays, in the 21st Century, the noise of powerful low flying fighter planes is very disturbing, if not positively frightening. I doubt if many people felt like that about the modest roar of twelve Spitfire pilots demonstrating their pride and joy in their machines at that date."[23]

During this stint at Westhampnett, 41 Squadron was in action almost every day as the Allies began gearing up for the forthcoming invasion of Europe. Indeed, it was part of this that, after the departure of 41 Squadron, there was a change in both aircraft and noise levels at Westhampnett with the arrival of 121 Wing of the 2nd Tactical Air Force.

Right: Two of 129 Squadron's groundcrew on Sergeant Ray Sherk's Spitfire at RAF Westhampnett in the summer of 1941. To the left of the squadron mascot, Jan, is Hopwell, whilst against the cockpit is Faulds. The aircraft is located on the airfield's southern boundary, the picture taken looking north towards the Downs. (Courtesy of Ray Sherk)

Opposite page: One of 129 Squadron's mascots, the Alsatian Jan, in the cockpit of one of its Spitfire Mk.Vbs, in this case that flown by Sergeant Ray Sherk. The picture was taken at RAF Westhampnett in August or September 1941. (Courtesy of Ray Sherk)

Left: Between December 1941 and March 1942, 41 Squadron was also based at Westhampnett alongside 129 Squadron. One of the former's Spitfires, which carried the squadron code letters of 'EB', forms the backdrop for a group photograph of some of its personnel. In the centre is the 41 Squadron's CO, Squadron Leader Petrus Hendrick 'Dutch' Hugo DFC & Bar. A South African, Hugo had flown Hurricanes in the Battle of Britain. To his left is Wing Commander Michael Lister Robinson who had flown with 601 (County of London) Squadron during the Battle of Britain. Robinson was shot down and killed on 10 April 1942, whilst leading the Tangmere Wing on a sweep over northern France. (Courtesy of the late Wing Commander Robert George 'Bob' Middlemiss, DFC, CD)

Left: A picture that was taken moments before, or after, the picture above left. Some of the pilots of 41 Squadron are seen standing around with the Wing Leader, Wing Commander Michael Robinson DSO, DFC. (Courtesy of the late Wing Commander Robert George 'Bob' Middlemiss, DFC, CD)

Above: Tangmere Wing Leader, Wing Commander Michael L. Robinson DSO, DFC, pictured with Sergeant Herbert 'Mitch' Mitchell of 41 Squadron at the dispersal hut at RAF Westhampnett in early 1942. Mitchell was a New Zealander and after service with 41 Squadron he was posted to 603 (City of Edinburgh) Squadron on Malta, from where he was flying when he was killed on 12 May 1942. He was aged just 25. (Courtesy of the late Wing Commander Robert George 'Bob' Middlemiss, DFC, CD)

Above: Squadron Leader Petrus Hendrik Hugo, 41 Squadron's CO, pictured at Westhampnett with a copy of the squadron's crest hanging around his neck. Hugo went on to be credited with seventeen kills, three shared, two unconfirmed destroyed, three probables and seven damaged. By the time he retired with the rank of Group Captain, he had been awarded a DFC and Bar, as well as the *Croix de Guerre* and an American DFC. (Courtesy of the late Wing Commander Robert George 'Bob' Middlemiss, DFC, CD)

Above: Sergeant Robert George Middlemiss pictured during a game of archery at Woodcote Farm. Middlemiss was promoted to Flight Sergeant in April 1942. (Courtesy of the late Wing Commander Robert George 'Bob' Middlemiss, DFC, CD)

Top right: A 41 Squadron Spitfire Mk.Vb being warmed up in the snow at Westhampnett. The trees in the background indicate that this picture was taken on the eastern side of the airfield. (Courtesy of the Swanwick Family via Steve Brew)

Right: Flight Lieutenant Thomas Fitzgerald, 41 Squadron's 'A' Flight commander, with his Spitfire. Fitzgerald was a New Zealander who had flown with 141 Squadron during the Battle of France and the Battle of Britain, being awarded the DFC in July 1940. (Courtesy of the Swanwick Family via Steve Brew)

This Page: Pilot Officer George Swanwick and Sergeant Herb Mitchell RNZAF, both of 41 Squadron, pictured during target practice behind the dispersal hut at Westhampnett. The bank in the background suggests that these pictures were taken on the airfield's western boundary. The other pilot present in the right-hand picture, wearing his Mae West, is Pilot Officer 'Kees' van Eendenburg. (Courtesy of the Swanwick Family via Steve Brew)

This page: A snow-covered 41 Squadron dispersal hut, in this case that of 'A' Flight, during the winter of 1941-1942. Note the squadron badge, which was adapted from the coat of arms of St Omer (this being the unit's first overseas base in 1916) marked out in the snow along with its motto, "Seek and Destroy". (Courtesy of the Swanwick Family via Steve Brew)

Above: Flying Officer John James 'Johnny' Allen RAAF with his Spitfire Mk.Vb on Westhampnett's eastern boundary. Allen made two claims for a damaged Fw 190 and a destroyed Bf 109F (shared) on 27 May 1942, but he was killed in a flying accident on 20 June 1942 aged just 22. (Courtesy of the Swanwick Family via Steve Brew)

Above: Pilot Officer Johnny Allen RAAF and 41 Squadron's Engineering Officer, Pilot Officer Roger 'Whippy' Whipp, standing in front of a Spitfire on Westhampnett's eastern boundary, just north of the entrance to the airfield as it is today. (Courtesy of the Swanwick Family via Steve Brew)

Above left: A 41 Squadron Mk.Vb, parked on a very snowy RAF Westhampnett during early 1942, adorned with a seasonal greeting for Adolf Hitler. (Courtesy of the Swanwick Family via Steve Brew)

Above right: Whilst 129 Squadron was still in residence at Westhampnett it was joined by the men and machines of 340 (Île-de-France) Squadron, a Free French unit which was also equipped with Mk.Vb Spitfires. The latter duly moved out for the Dieppe Raid. The Spitfires are carrying the vertical white bands on the engine cowlings which were applied for the Dieppe Raid. The distinctive water tower of Graylingwell Hospital can be seen in the background, telling us that these Spitfires were parked on the perimeter track at the airfield's south-east corner. (Critical Past)

French groundcrew work on the Spitfire Mk.Vb of
Commandant Bernard Dupérier of 340 (Île-de-France) Squadron.
His aircraft, BM324 coded 'GW-S', was adorned with
distinctive Daffy Duck nose art. On the day of the Dieppe
Raid Dupérier flew four support missions and
shared one destroyed bomber and one
damaged. (Critical Past)

Left: A 340 (Île-de-France) Squadron pilot preparing for the off. Note the Cross of Loraine on the cowling. Behind you can see The Trundle, this being the site of an Iron Age hill fort. The buildings behind are on the northern boundary of the airfield. (Critical Past)

Opposite: Spitfire Mk.Vbs of 340 (Île-de-France) Squadron at dispersal on the eastern boundary at Westhampnett being worked on by French groundcrew. After Westhampnett the squadron was posted to RAF Hornchurch. (Critical Past)

Above: One of 340 (Île-de-France) Squadron's pilots, Marcel Albert, in Spitfire EN908 which was coded 'GW-Y'. This aircraft was usually the personal mount of Emile Fayolle, the 'B' Flight commander. (Critical Past)

Opposite: Aircraft of 340 (Île-de-France) Squadron at dispersal on Westhampnett's western boundary, looking into the Lavant valley beyond. The same Duty Pilot hut can be seen in some of the 129 Squadron photographs. (Critical Past)

Below: Spitfire Mk.Vbs of 340 (Île-de-France) Squadron parked on the southern perimeter track. Further Spitfires can be seen parked in the fields behind, indicating that the wartime airfield covered more land than it does today. The dog running around the track, visible to the right of the image, is probably Jan the Alsatian of 129 Squadron. (Critical Past)

Opposite: A pilot of the US 309th Fighter Squadron prepares to start the Merlin of his Spitfire Mk.Vb with the aid of a 'Trolly Acc', or trolley accumulator. This photograph was taken on the eastern boundary of the airfield near Fishers Cottage. (Critical Past)

Left: The Duchess of Gloucester (on the left) pictured during a visit to Westhampnett's communal site at Westerton in July 1942. This site, which was known officially as Communal Site No.1, had a ration store, grocery store, and sergeants' and officers' messes. Some of the buildings can still be seen behind the village and at least one of the brick and concrete shelters is still visible. (Courtesy of Tangmere Military Aviation Museum)

Below: Spitfire Mk.Vb 'WZ-A', which was the personal mount of Major Harrison Thyng of the 309th, at Westhampnett. Thyng went on to become an Ace during the war, as well as a jet Ace whilst flying the F-86 Sabre in Korea. (Critical Past)

Opposite: A Hawker Typhoon 1b of 56 Squadron pictured taking off from Westhampnett in early June 1942. The aircraft is being flown by the squadron's Commanding Officer, Squadron Leader 'Cocky' Dundas, who had previously been at Westhampnett in 1941 whilst serving with 616 (South Yorkshire) Squadron. After formation at RAF Duxford, one of 56 Squadron's two flights was posted to RAF Manston, the other to Westhampnett to patrol the coast. (Critical Past)

Below: A Spitfire Mk.Vb of the 309th Fighter Squadron, coded 'WZ-E', parked at dispersal with the Trundle in the background to the north. The 309th arrived at Westhampnett on 4 August 1942. (Critical Past)

Above and Below: Spitfires Mk.Vbs of the 309th Fighter Squadron landing at Westhampnett. The Americans were part of the 31st Fighter Wing and the airfield, identified as Station 352, was handed over to the US Eighth Air Force. As well as participating in the Dieppe Raid, the 309th's Spitfires also flew bomber escort sorties and carried out standing patrols from Westhampnett. (Critical Past)

Left: Lieutenant Harry Strawn in the cockpit of his 309th Fighter Squadron Spitfire, coded 'WZ-X', which he nicknamed *Beverley*. Strawn saw action in Europe and in North Africa flying Spitfires. He was shot down by flak and wounded but was later returned to the USA, volunteering to fly the Republic P-47 Thunderbolt in the Far East. He was awarded the Air Medal for his bravery. (Courtesy of Nancy Strawn Adams)

Above: Major Harrison Thyng in the cockpit of his Spitfire at the dispersal on the eastern boundary. Thyng used to sit in his cockpit for up to five hours at a time waiting for any action. Although not initially popular with his men he soon earned their respect over Dieppe. (Courtesy of Nancy Strawn Adams)

Above: Major Harrison Thyng (on the left) stands in front of a dispersal hut with the squadron badge on the door. The other two officers are Lieutenant Tharpe and Lieutenant Cogwin (on the right), the Engineering Officer. (Courtesy of Nancy Strawn Adams)

Right: A view of the 309th Fighter Squadron's 'B' Flight dispersal at Westhampnett. In the rear row, left to right, are pilots Lieutenant Sam Junkin, Lieutenant Bill Bryson, 1st Lieutenant Dale Schafer, and Lieutenant Emil Tanassy. Initially the Americans had no motor transport so they relied on bicycles to get about. (Courtesy of Nancy Strawn Adams)

Both pages: A sequence of photographs taken in August 1942 showing Lieutenant Bob Weismuller putting on his Mae West and parachute before climbing into his Spitfire at 'B' Flight's dispersal. Note 309th Fighter Squadron's code letters of 'WZ' on the fuselage. Weismuller went on to fly the Bell P-39 Aircobra in North Africa, an aircraft he had trained on in the USA prior to conversion to the Spitfire. (Courtesy of Nancy Strawn Adams)

Right: Lieutenant 'Spike' Schofield of the 309th with his Spitfire Mk.Vb nicknamed *Phyllis*. The Americans regarded the Spitfire highly. 'Spike' Schofield was Harry Strawn's Blackjack partner. (Courtesy of Nancy Strawn Adams)

Below: Lieutenant Bob Weismuller standing at dispersal wearing his USAAF uniform and garrison hat. Typically the pilots would all wear A2 leather jackets with a shirt and tie underneath whilst at the dispersal; the uniform seem here was kept for best and parades. (Courtesy of Nancy Strawn Adams)

Above: Captain Winfred 'Salty' Chambers sat in the cockpit of Spitfire Mk.Vb 'WZ-L', which was the usual mount of Lieutenant Sam Junkin. 'Salty' Chambers was to be killed in a flying accident at Westhampnett on 1 October 1942. At the time he was performing low-level aerobatics below 500 feet. (Courtesy of Nancy Strawn Adams)

Above right: Lieutenant Samuel Junkin reading a paper on the steps of Fishers Cottage prior to the Dieppe Raid. He became the 309th Fighter Squadron's first combat casualty on that day, receiving cannon shell injuries to his right shoulder. He baled out of his aircraft after having trouble with his cockpit hood and was eventually picked up by an RAF air sea rescue launch. However, prior to being injured he was credited with a Focke-Wulf Fw 190, thereby becoming the first of the USAAF's Eighth Air Force fighter pilots to make a claim. (Courtesy of Nancy Strawn Adams)

Left: A few weeks after arriving at Westhampnett, the 309th Fighter Squadron's transport started to arrive. Here three of the squadron pilots prepare for a night out in the local area – they used to frequent dances in Chichester and Bognor Regis. The Jeep is parked outside Fishers Cottage where Lieutenant Harry Strawn was accommodated. (Courtesy of Nancy Strawn Adams)

Above: Lieutenant D.K. Smith of the 309th observes the damage that a 20mm cannon shell has done to his port wing during sorties in support of the Dieppe Raid on 19 August 1942. All three of the squadrons making up the 31st Fighter Wing took part. (Courtesy of D. Kucera)

Above: Whilst on leave in London, Lieutenant Harry Strawn (on the left) purchased a dog and brought it back with him to his accommodation at Westhampnett – and more specifically Fishers Cottage. Here the young puppy, named Red, is seen with Harry and another of the 309th's pilots. (Courtesy of Nancy Strawn Adams)

Right: The 309th Fighter Squadron's Captain Winfred 'Salty' Chambers outside Fishers Cottage. (Courtesy of Nancy Strawn Adams)

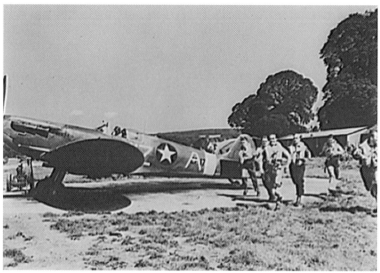

Left: Lieutenant Bob Barber of the 309th Fighter Squadron at Fishers Cottage. (Courtesy of Nancy Strawn Adams)

Above: A staged photograph of some of the 309th's pilots during a scramble. The aircraft, Spitfire 'WZ-A', was the personal mount of Major H. Thyng. This picture was taken on the airfield's eastern boundary, just north of Fishers Cottage. (Courtesy of Nancy Strawn Adams)

Opposite: A photograph of pilots of 'B' Flight of the 308th Fighter Squadron, which moved into Westhampnett alongside the 309th. The 307th Fighter Squadron went to nearby Merston. The 308th Spitfires carried the squadron code letters 'HL'. (Courtesy of D. Kucera)

Opposite: Lieutenant 'Happy' Chandler, Lieutenant Norman Thompson and Lieutenant Peter Payne, all of the 309th, pose for a photograph at Westhampnett in September 1942. All three men were regular poker players and could often be found at Woodcote Farm playing personnel from 'A' Flight. (Courtesy of D. Kucera)

Above: Pilot Officer Doug Brown with his 485 Squadron Spitfire, a Mk.Vb nicknamed *Wine, Women & Song*, at RAF Westhampnett. Brown later became 'A' Flight's commander and subsequently posted to 130 Squadron. (Courtesy of Doug Brown)

Right: A 307th Fighter Squadron Spitfire stands outside the T2 hangar at Westhampnett. This is the earliest known photograph of this structure and was probably taken in September or October 1942. This hangar still survives to the north of the current airfield. (Courtesy of D. Kucera)

Opposite: The three men in this picture are, from left to right: Flight Lieutenant John Pattison RNZAF, Squadron Leader Reginald Grant DFC, DFM, and Flight Lieutenant Reginald Baker, all of whom were serving with 485 (NZ) Squadron. Pattison had flown with Nos. 92 and 266 squadrons during the Battle of Britain; he was shot down by a Bf 109 in September 1940 and badly wounded. He joined 485 Squadron in April 1942. Grant was killed later in the war whilst baling out too low from a Mustang in 1944. Baker, the 'A' Flight commander when this picture was taken, would take over as 485's CO on 20 March 1943. He was to be killed in action on 22 February 1945 whilst flying a de Havilland Mosquito as the CO of 487 (NZ) Squadron. (Courtesy of the late Doug Brown)

Above left: Some of 485 Squadron's pilots entertaining one evening at Fishers Cottage. Squadron Leader Reginald Grant DFC, DFM can be seen at left rear. (Courtesy of the late Doug Brown)

Above: The aftermath of one of the many parties at RAF Westhampnett. The upper floor windows of Fishers Cottage have been left open to vent the smoke from a fire which was accidentally started by the revellers. (Courtesy of the late Doug Brown)

Opposite: No.485 (NZ) Squadron's Flight Lieutenant J. Pattison recounting a combat to Squadron Leader 'Reg' Grant (on the left) and Flight Lieutenant R. Baker (right). (IWM; CH008385)

Above: Groundcrew of 485 (NZ) Squadron relax at dispersal in front of one of the squadron's Mk.Vb Spitfires. This image was taken on the south-east corner of the airfield, looking north-west with the South Downs in the background. The Spitfire in the centre is sitting on a stretch of the perimeter track that still exists today as the part of the race track known as Madgwick Corner. (Author's Collection)

Above: Personnel of both Nos. 41 and 91 squadrons outside one of the dispersal huts at RAF Westhampnett. (Courtesy of the late Peter Graham)

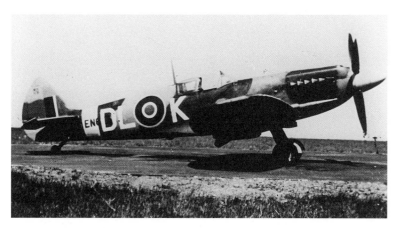

Above: A Spitfire Mk.XII of 91 (Nigeria) Squadron, coded 'DL-K'. No.91 Squadron joined 41 Squadron at RAF Westhampnett. Led by Wing Commander Rhys Thomas, the newly-formed Spitfire XII Wing carried out its first joint mission on 29 June 1942, a *Ramrod* escorting Flying Fortresses to Le Mans. During July the Tangmere Wing continued to be primarily engaged in *Ramrods* – escorting more Fortresses, as well as Mitchells, Marauders and Typhoons, to targets in France. (Courtesy of Andrew Thomas)

Right: Flight Lieutenant Arthur 'Pinky' Glenn. Glenn, who later went on to command 41 Squadron in January 1944, was at Westhampnett in 1942 with the same squadron and was awarded a DFC for three victories. He was posted to 603 (City of Edinburgh) Squadron on Malta, flying off from HMS *Eagle*. He claimed a further three victories on 6 July 1942. Shortly after he was injured by a bomb blast and returned to the UK. He was awarded a Bar to his DFC in 1943. (Courtesy of the late Peter Graham)

Left: Flight Lieutenant Lord Gisborough was 41 Squadron's Intelligence Officer. Thomas Weston Peel Long Chaloner, the Rt. Hon. Lord Gisborough, 2nd Baron Gisborough of Cleveland, was a former Royal Flying Corps pilot who had been shot down on 1 July 1916, the first day of the Battle of the Somme, and spent the rest of the First World War as a prisoner of war. (Courtesy of the late Peter Graham)

Above: Pilot Officer Peter Graham was a flight sergeant pilot whilst flying the Spitfire Mk.XII from RAF Westhampnett. On one sortie he suffered serious damage to his aircraft, but opted to return to his home airfield rather than divert to nearby RAF Tangmere, which had far better crash facilities. (Courtesy of the late Peter Graham)

In October 1943 three Typhoon squadrons, Nos. 174 (Mauritius), 175 and 245 (Northern Rhodesia), arrived at Westhampnett as part of 121 Airfield of the 2nd Tactical Air Force's No.83 Group.

Both 174 and 175 squadrons had been formed in March 1942 as fighter-bomber units equipped with Hurricane IIbs. They converted to Typhoons in 1943 and were to provide invaluable ground support to the army during and after D-Day. For its part, 245 Squadron was originally formed as a Blenheim unit in 1939, later converting to Hurricanes. It also took on the fighter-bomber role in 1943 and converted to Typhoons.

At this stage of the war the Hawker Typhoon was still suffering from both misidentification by other Allied pilots – from a distance it could be mistaken for a Focke-Wulf Fw 190 – and engine failures, the Napier Sabre 24-cylinder H-block engine being an extremely complicated piece of engineering. An example of misidentification involving a Westhampnett-based Typhoon occurred in November 1944 when Flying Officer Diggins of 175 Squadron was attacked by a Spitfire whilst operating over France. Diggins made a 'wheels-up' landing at Tangmere. The mechanical problems, meanwhile,

Previous page: A queue for the NAAFI tea van at the dispersal area at Westhampnett, the backdrop being provided by one of 245 (Northern Rhodesia) Squadron's Typhoons. Note the aircraft's bubble canopy, this type having replaced the original heavy-framed example, which provided a greatly improved field of view. A de Havilland Tiger Moth, the squadron's 'hack', can just be made out on the left of the picture. (IWM; CH12249)

Opposite: Armourers load a 500lb bomb on to a Hawker Typhoon Mk.IB, JP802 coded 'MR-M', of 245 (Northern Rhodesia) Squadron at Westhampnett, 18 January 1944. The Typhoon squadrons arrived at Westhampnett in October 1943 when Nos. 174, 175 and 245 squadrons flew in as part of the 2nd Tactical Air Force. (IWM; CH12252)

led to the loss of Flight Lieutenant Black's 174 Squadron aircraft when he crashed not far from Alfriston, East Sussex, in December 1943.

The majority of Typhoon missions at the end of 1943 involved sweeps over northern France, the pilots attacking targets of opportunity, though bad weather curtailed operations during December. As the New Year broke the squadrons at Westhampnett continued with *Ramrods*. An example of this type of sortie was *Ramrod* 440 on 8 January 1944. This sweep was to be to the north of Paris and was led by Wing Commander Robert Davidson DFC.[1] There were two squadrons taking part – Nos. 174 and 245 – with a total of fourteen Typhoons.

The participating aircraft took off at 13.11 hours. Heading out over Beachy Head, they flew on to France at a height of 8,000 feet. Near Compiègne Davidson spotted an enemy aircraft which, accompanied by Pilot Officer Dickie, he attacked from astern. Davidson gave it a burst of fire from a range of 500 yards, closing down to 100 yards. The aircraft, then identified as a French Lioré-et-Olivier LeO 45 medium bomber, was seen to drop its undercarriage as one wing disintegrated.

As the squadrons passed over the *Luftwaffe* airfield at Brétigny-sur-Orge, a suburb of Paris, five Junkers Ju 88s were seen on the airfield, with one coming in to land. This landing aircraft was promptly attacked and observed to crash outside the airfield boundary. Yet another was seen above the airfield at Guyancourt and this time strikes were seen on the fuselage as black smoke belched from it. The Typhoons broke off and, as they looked back, this enemy bomber was also seen to crash. Another Ju 88 was encountered near Bornay, and two pilots from 245 Squadron engaged it. However, one of the pair, Flight Sergeant Bill Waudby in JP971, was shot down.[2] A number of the Typhoons also engaged in attacking military transports before returning home to Westhampnett.

As well as being involved in attacking *Noball* targets – these were raids intended to destroy V-1 flying bomb installations, such as launch sites –

carrying 500lb bombs, the Westhampnett Typhoons also found themselves involved in Operation *Jericho*, the raid on Amiens prison on 18 February 1944.

The objective of the mission was to attack the prison in an attempt to assist 120 prisoners, many whom were members of the Resistance, to escape. The pilots of the first attacking wave had been briefed to bomb, and breach, the outer wall in two places, whilst the second was to target the main building and guards' quarters. Following ten minutes behind, the third wave was a reserve to be utilised if any part of the initial objectives had not been met. A single Photographic Reconnaissance Unit de Havilland Mosquito, flown by Flight Lieutenant Tony Wickham, would record events.

Three formations totalling eighteen Mosquitoes were each accompanied by Typhoons as close support. The Westhampnett-based 174 Squadron was one of the units selected for the latter role.

The attackers flew out over Littlehampton in atrocious weather, scudding beneath low cloud and snow. Fortunately the skies cleared as the raiders ran in over the French coast. Each formation then split up into two sections of three aircraft. The Mosquitoes approached the target at sixty feet and, with airspeed indicators passing 350mph, each aircraft dropped four 500lb bombs. The third wave was not needed and returned with its bomb load intact.

Flying Officer Frank Wheeler of 174 Squadron was one of the pilots flying that day: "I arrived at Westhampnett to join 174 Squadron at the end of January 1944. The squadron was part of 121 Wing, Second Tactical Air Force, with the other Squadrons being 175 and 245. Almost immediately the squadron moved to Eastchurch Armament Training Camp where, for the first time, we were introduced to rocket projectiles.

"On returning to Westhampnett in February the weather made flying difficult and I had not flown my first operational sortie. February 16th and 17th found us sitting around the dispersal hut at the edge of the field while snow and blizzards swept over southern England. On the 18th there were signs of improvement and my Flight Commander, Flight Lieutenant Grantham, suddenly appeared and announced there was a show on today and, looking at me, said, 'You are flying number two to me'.

"We went to briefing and realised that this was something different and special. During the winter of 1943 and 1944 the Germans had managed to infiltrate some of the Resistance groups in the Amiens area. This resulted in a large number of arrests and imprisonments in the political wing of the Amiens prison. This wing was run by the Gestapo. The sentence for being a member of the Resistance was death and a large number of prisoners awaited death by firing squad.

"140 Mosquito Wing at Hunsdon had become adept at low-level raids with particular skill not only in flying but also in navigation and bomb placing. Group Captain Pickard had recently become Commanding Officer of 140 Wing, joined, of course, by his Navigator Flight Lieutenant Broadley. The Wing would carry out a raid on the Amiens prison with 487 (New Zealand) Squadron to breach the outer wall, 464 (Australian) Squadron to place bombs on the German quarters and 21 Squadron as a reserve. Each squadron was to have a Typhoon escort.

"The Germans had built on their own accommodation at the end of the prison. It was known that most of the German staff would be at these two areas for lunch at 12:00 hours. 487 were briefed to attack the outer walls at 12:00 hours, 464 to attack the German quarters at 12:03 and 21 Squadron to be ready if needed. 464 were told to place their bombs as close as possible to the main walls to ensure that doors would be rattled of their hinges. 609 Squadron Typhoons were to escort 487, 174 and 245 from Westhampnett were to escort 464 and 21 Squadrons respectively…

Opposite: Having bombed-up a 245 (Northern Rhodesia) Squadron Typhoon, groundcrew add a suitable message for its recipients. (IWM CH12251)

"We took off, formed up and arrived at Littlehampton, the rendezvous, in a few minutes. North of the South Downs was very murky and 464 were not able to safely form up. They arrived line astern, first four, then three more. When we reached the coast it was clear for them to get into formation.

"Number seven to arrive was the photographic reconnaissance Mosquito that was considered to be of great importance. Red 3 and 4 of 174 escorted the filming unit throughout the operation. Tony Wickham, the [PRU] pilot, was reported as having said to his navigator, 'I'm sure if we go down a railway tunnel, they'll come right down with us'.

"We crossed the channel at 'nought' feet. On reaching the French coast we flew at tree top or roof top height. The route was not directly to Amiens prison but a wide ranging circuit to the right, eventually meeting the Albert-Amiens road. This road runs north-east/south-west and gave a straight route to the prison, which is actually situated on this road.

"Before reaching the target the second section of 3 broke away to the right and attacked from the north, while the first section of three came in from the north-east. We could see the piles of rubble where the New Zealanders had successfully breached the outer wall. One gap can still be discerned today by the different colours of the infilling brickwork.

"464 Squadron now took their turn and planted their bombs with skill and accuracy. Having done their job they sped for home. We were not briefed to escort them back but Red 3 and 4 escorted the PRU Mosquito back to the English coast, after Tony Wickham had made three runs over the target to get a film of people escaping.

"Our leader called over the intercom for [Flight Lieutenant] Ian Mallett and his section to join us and move north to attack barges on the Seine. Ian Mallett said that this was not possible as they would not have enough fuel. They were given permission to return to base. The weather began to worsen and heavy snow clouds appeared, some reaching ground level.

"Ian Mallett's flight of four met this weather and continued flying on instruments. When they emerged from the gloom Ian's number 2, Pilot

Opposite: Pilots of 245 (Northern Rhodesia) Squadron walk past their Typhoon Mk.IBs towards their dispersal hut at Westhampnett. They have just returned from an attack against a V-1 flying-bomb launch site in northern France – a so-called *Noball* target. Three of the Typhoons wear cowling covers with 'chimneys' for the insertion of a heater to aid the engine start. In the background is a Hawker Hurricane which was used by the squadron as a communications and training aircraft. The pilots are walking along a stretch of the perimeter track on the south-east corner of the airfield which is now known as Madgwick Corner and forms part of the modern-day race track. The track notes for the racing circuit state that, "The first corner after the pits, Madgwick, is a fast, sweeping right-handler with a double apex". The men in this picture include Bob Lee (second from the left) who would go on to survive five days in an upturned Typhoon near Mortain. The other pilots are John Hampson, Roly Temple, 'Which' Martin, John Golley, Sheep Milne and Nobby Clark. (IWM; CH12255A)

Officer Renault, had been shot down – but survived the crash and became a PoW.

"21 Squadron waited for the signal to either attack or return to base. The return to base order was received but there is doubt as to whether Group Captain Pickard gave the order or Tony Wickham. Nothing further was heard from Pickard – he and his navigator, Flight Lieutenant Broadley, had been shot down and killed.

"Flight Lieutenant Grantham found our barges, which we attacked with little effect. To my relief we also set course for base but found ourselves facing thick snow clouds. Grantham waggled his wings, which meant close up, which I did, but as soon as we entered cloud he disappeared. During briefing we had been given a course to steer for the nearest home base. I had written this in ink on the back of my left hand. I turned on to this course and kept going.

Above: Armourers cleaning the barrels of a 245 (Northern Rhodesia) Squadron Typhoon's four 20mm Hispano Mk.II cannon, 18 January 1944. The aircraft is JR311, coded 'MR-G'. (IWM; CH12253)

"Near the coast the weather improved. I guessed that there would be coastal flak so went from land to sea fast and low. There were a few splashes in the water but I was clear and crossing the Channel. My fuel was quite low.

"Nearing the English coast I saw nothing familiar but miracles do happen. I saw something, which was the answer to my problems – a windsock. In no time I had landed and taxied in. I was met by a Flight Lieutenant and a number of groundcrew. 'What was the landing like?' they asked. I said it was fine and was told that I had landed on a steel mesh runway at Lydd which had just been put down and I was the first to land on it. The Flight Lieutenant was busy on a field telephone and he informed me that my flight commander had just landed at Hawkinge. I was to join him there for a de-briefing. Ten minutes later, having had my aircraft refuelled, I was at Hawkinge.

"My flight commander and I were debriefed in a room at flying control. The intelligence officer was asking a series of questions which Grantham answered. Eventually he asked if either of us seen anyone escape. I replied that I had. 'What was he wearing?' I replied, 'He was a big man, clambering over the rubble. He must have been the boiler man, he was wearing dungarees.' For the first time the intelligence officer smiled. I did not know that all the prisoners wore blue overalls!

"We stayed the night at Hawkinge where I had a meal but I was not carrying any money. I had a free night in the Sergeants' Mess so had a couple of pints and slept well that night despite snow dripping through the roof of my room.

"Next morning we were up for an early breakfast and flew back along the South Downs in glorious sunshine. We arrived [at Westhampnett] in time for another breakfast! That made my day."[3]

On 22 March 1944, a new type of aircraft arrived at Westhampnett in the shape of the North American P-51 Mustang. Two Mustang Mk.Is from 168 Squadron, carrying out photographic reconnaissance duties, were posted on detachment from Gatwick for just three days.

Another change saw 121 Airfield and the Typhoons transfer out of Westhampnett to RAF Holmsley South, Hampshire, at the end of March. It was not the last time that Typhoons operated from Westhampnett, however, as they returned with 184 Squadron in April, as part of the lead up to D-Day, and 83 Group Support Unit at the end of 1944.

Above: A Westhampnett-based 174 Squadron Typhoon, JP535 'XP-A' flown by Flying Officer Harry Markby, pictured in close formation with de Havilland Mosquito DZ414, which was being piloted by Flight Lieutenant Wickham. This photograph was taken on 18 February 1944, when Nos. 174 and 245 squadrons provided the escort for the Mosquitoes participating in the raid on Amiens prison. Only 174 Squadron managed to escort the bombers all the way from Westhampnett. Two of its pilots, Flying Officer J.E. Reynaud and Flight Sergeant H. Brown, did not return; Reynaud became a PoW whilst Brown was killed. (245 Squadron Archive, via Chris Thomas)

Above: Flight Lieutenant Arthur Eugene 'Ace' Miron RCAF, of 245 (Northern Rhodesia) Squadron, with his Typhoon, JP650, probably in March 1944. Still standing today, the cottages in the background are those at the north-east corner of Westhampnett airfield near the current crash gate No.13. (245 Squadron Archive, via Chris Thomas)

D-DAY AND BEYOND

As D-Day approached, the changes at Westhampnett came thick and fast. At the beginning of April 1944, for example, three Canadian units, Nos. 441 (Silver Fox), 442 (Caribou) and 443 (Hornet) squadrons, moved in, all three being equipped with Spitfire Mk.IXs. As well as completing their training for the forthcoming invasion, all three squadrons were tasked with undertaking sweeps over northern France. They did not remain long, departing to RAF Funtington, just to the north-west of Westhampnett, towards the end of April.

The next unit to fly in was 184 Squadron, which remained at Westhampnett until after D-Day. During the Normandy landings its role was to provide air support over the beachheads. Indeed, 184 Squadron carried out a number of sorties in direct support of Operation *Overlord*, one of which proved particularly costly.

On 7 June 1944, D+1, the squadron undertook a rocket attack on the railway marshalling yards at Mézidon-Canon. Encountering strong German resistance and heavy anti-aircraft fire, three of the eight Typhoons from Westhampnett were shot down. One of the pilots, Flight Sergeant J.J. Rowland (at the controls of JP656) was killed. Fight Sergeant L. Tidbury (MN642), on the other hand, was taken prisoner, whilst Flight Lieutenant F.E. Holland (MN667) evaded capture and was on the run for seventy days before making it back to Allied lines.

Previous page: When 303 (Polish) Squadron arrived at Westhampnett after D-Day they were still flying the Spitfire Mk.Vb, although these were soon replaced by the Mk.IXF variant. Here, Flight Lieutenant Bruno Kudrewicz stands in front of his Mk.Vb. He was posted to the squadron in January 1944 and left on 6 July the same year having been posted to 84 Group Support Unit. He is credited with having destroyed two aircraft, and damaged one, during his service career. He survived the war and emigrated to New Zealand. (Via P. Sikora)

Flight Lieutenant Frank 'Dutch' Holland later recalled having taken off from Westhampnett at 15.50 hours to conduct "an armed patrol in the Falaise [*sic*] area":

"The first hiccup came a few minutes into the flight when Sam Jessee, who had been in both the previous sorties, reported some mechanical difficulty and had to turn back. But the immediate problem was the weather, the lack of good visibility. When you have a known target, you have the compass bearings from base, the approximate distance, and your flight speed, but there is always uncertainty.

"We flew over the Channel at 1,000 feet, round Le Havre, then south towards Mézidon. Like the other missions that day, this was a *Rhubarb* – we were just looking for any and all German military targets that we might hit.

"About 20-25 minutes into the flight, we passed over some marshalling yards in the town of Mézidon. We were going at 350-380 miles an hour and I missed the sight at first but suddenly there was a radio contact from one of the pilots, who shouted out 'Did you see that below?' The marshalling yards were just below, a huge concentration of rolling stock, tanks on flat cars, troop carriers, jeeps, you name it, plus lots of German troops."[1]

The last-minute sighting of this target meant that the Typhoon pilots were unable to make an immediate attack so they devised a plan to deceive the Germans by continuing to fly to the south before rapidly turning back in the hope of taking the enemy by surprise. Consequently, ten minutes later the pilots executed a sharp turn and, reversing course, rapidly lost altitude and increased their speed.

"I was in the lead," continued Holland, "and as we approached, I was close enough to see the eyes of the soldiers manning the anti-aircraft guns. They were waiting for us. They had known we would be back and had been expecting us. The firing started as we made our approach. My aircraft was hit even before firing off my first rockets."[2]

Frank 'Dutch' Holland's Typhoon was losing glycol and the engine temperature was rising rapidly. He was too low to bale out. As he climbed in an effort to gain height to attempt a jump, Holland found his hood was stuck. After a few heart-stopping moments spent freeing it, he eventually escaped from his cockpit. He survived the jump, going on the run through Normandy.

During the period of the D-Day landings another of the airmen based at Westhampnett was Pilot Officer Evan Bumford. Bumford, however, was not a pilot serving with a Typhoon squadron – he flew a Taylorcraft Auster military liaison and observation aircraft as part of 84 Group's communications flight. He was billeted in tents in the woods to the north of the airfield, beyond what is now the racing circuit's Lavant Straight.

At that time the Group's headquarters had moved into the grounds of Goodwood House, although the house itself was also home to doctors and nurses of a field hospital, whilst the majority of its radio equipment was located on the racecourse. Bumford recalls how he would often fly his Auster up to the Trundle and land on the home straight of the racecourse itself. His unit crossed the Channel to northern France in August 1944.[3]

It was during June 1944 that Spitfire squadrons returned to Westhampnett. Amongst these was 130 (Punjab) Squadron, one of whose pilots was Flight Lieutenant Doug Brown, who had already spent time at Westhampnett in

Right: Squadron Leader T. Koc DFC, who was the Commanding Officer of 303 (Polish) Squadron whilst it was based at Westhampnett, pictured during the D-Day period. His squadron flew a variety of sorties from the airfield, including providing air cover for shipping, *Ramrods* and low-level support for troops in the Caen area. Koc relinquished command on 24 September 1944, being posted to 61 Operational Training Unit. (Via P. Sikora)

1943 whilst serving with 485 (NZ) Squadron. Brown later recalled his second period at this West Sussex airfield:

"The squadron was posted from RAF Horne in Surrey to Westhampnett on 20 June 1944 and moved on to RAF Merston on 27 June 1944. It was early August when we subsequently converted to the Spitfire Mk.XIV at Tangmere. Our Commanding Officer at the time was Bill Ireson and I was a flight commander with Scotty Scott.

"When we moved back in the Officers' accommodation was Shopwyke House, originally a school and post-war reverted back to that role. During the six days there, we basically carried out beachhead patrols over Normandy."[4]

The Poles also returned to Westhampnett in June 1944, when 303 (Polish) Squadron flew in on the 19th – an advance party of groundcrew and mechanics had arrived the previous day to prepare the airfield. On arrival 303 Squadron was operating Spitfire Mk.Vbs, though these were soon replaced by the Mk.IXc.

Left: Flight Lieutenant Józef Stasik sat in his Spitfire; note the distinctive squadron emblem. Stasik joined the RAF in 1941, attending 58 Operational Training Unit before being posted to 308 (Polish) Squadron on 20 March 1942. He arrived at 303 (Polish) Squadron in October of that year and quickly started to make his mark, claiming two Focke-Wulf Fw 190s destroyed and a further one damaged. On 11 August 1944, Stasik and other 303 (Polish) Squadron pilots escorted a B-25 Mitchell transporting the Supreme Commander Allied Forces in Europe, General Dwight D. Eisenhower, to Airfield A.9 in Normandy. On 31 August 1944, Stasik was participating in an armed reconnaissance mission to the Hardelot area, having taken off from Westhampnett, when his Spitfire, MH882, was shot down by anti-aircraft fire whilst he was attacking an enemy column. Stasik was killed. (Via P. Sikora)

Right: Flying Officer Witold Aleksander Herbst of 303 (Polish) Squadron was shot down whilst flying a sortie in support of Operation *Market Garden* on 17 September 1944. His squadron's role was to provide close fighter escort and neutralize the flak for a force of sixty-seven Stirlings. Led by Wing Commander John 'Johnny' Milne Checketts DSO, DFC, seven Spitfire Mk.IXFs took off from RAF Manston (to where they had forward-deployed from Westhampnett) at 12.50 hours, reaching Arnhem at 14.10 hours. Herbst's aircraft was hit by flak and he baled out over northern France. (Via P. Sikora)

The Poles were to have a busy time at Westhampnett, not only providing cover over the D-Day beaches from D+13 but also supporting the airborne landings of Operation *Market Garden* at Arnhem in September 1944. At this stage the squadron was being led by Squadron Leader Tadeusz Koc DFC.

One of those who remembers this period was Flying Officer Witold A. Herbst: "On D-Day I had flown myself three sorties and was astonished by the absence of the *Luftwaffe*. We were patrolling the beaches for nearly two weeks when the Germans launched their V-1 attack. There was something of a panic everywhere but in a matter of days anti-aircraft artillery was brought in from all over England and deployed south of London. These damned things [the flying bombs] flew over our heads day and night; anti-aircraft batteries were all around us and the continuous din had an effect on us – we never slept with this concert going on around us.

"We [initially] moved to Tangmere on June 20, where we stayed a couple of days while I suppose Westhampnett was being prepared to receive us. From Westhampnett we were still patrolling the beaches for a few days but having been rearmed with Spitfire Mk.IXs we started escorting bombers again; these were blasting communication centres deep into France."[5]

Perhaps because of the frantic activity surrounding Operation *Overlord* there were a number of accidents at Westhampnett in this period. On 21 June, for example, 303 Squadron's Flight Sergeant J. Talar returned to the airfield from a sortie at about 00.05 hours. As he touched down the starboard undercarriage leg on his Spitfire collapsed, with the net result that both wheels folded, though Talar was uninjured. Two months later he was to have yet another 'prang' whilst landing a Spitfire Mk.IX in a crosswind; the aircraft 'ground-looped' and tipped on to its nose.

On 23 June 1944, 303 Squadron lost one of its top scoring pilots, Warrant Officer A. Chudek. He was flying Spitfire AB271, 'RF-F', on a routine patrol over Normandy when he was shot down and killed. He had claimed nine victories and one 'probable' in his career as a fighter pilot, being awarded the DFM, the Polish *Virtuti Militari* 5th Class and a Cross of Valour with four Bars.

In late July, 303 Squadron moved the short distance to Merston, though when they returned on 9 August they were allocated the important task of escorting a B-25 Mitchell carrying the Allied Supreme Commander, General Dwight D. Eisenhower to Airfield A.9 in Normandy. The squadron also returned to *Ramrod* and *Rodeo* sorties, as well as occasionally providing a close escort to Martin B-26 Marauders.

Flying Officer Witold A. Herbst recalls one of the long range sorties undertaken at this time: "I remember one escort that we did to Joigny, some 80-100 miles south of Paris. I remember this one clearly: about 80 Lancasters dropped their considerable load on the railway lines all around the town which disappeared in a mountain of smoke. We were astonished to learn later that the town was practically intact."

At the end of August the squadron participated in *Ramrod* 1236, escorting a force of 200 Halifaxes on a raid against fuel dumps at Homberg. On the way in to the target, Red Section saw an aircraft dive down out of the sun and rapidly passed through the formation. Two of the Spitfire pilots took a snap shot at this aircraft but no hits were seen. It later

transpired that the Poles had observed a Messerschmitt Me 163 *Komet*, one of Germany's new secret weapons. Flying Officer Herbst recalled this unusual encounter:

"On August 26 we escorted bombers to Homburg, south of Münster, and on this occasion I saw German jets for the first time. At first there was a single aircraft hanging over us. I took my foursome away from the squadron and looked with astonishment at this thing beginning to dive, a Messerschmitt 163. I managed to give it a short salvo and went after him. Unfortunately the German pilot kept his dive or was hit, I will never know, and at 10,000 feet my windscreen started to ice up and I had to pull out. I claimed it as damaged."[6]

This mission was closely followed by *Ramrod* 1250 on 31 August. In this, 303 Squadron was to provide target cover to five groups of Lancasters on a *Noball* sortie in the St Omer area. This involved twelve Spitfire Mk.IXFs led by Squadron Leader Koc.

Later that afternoon 303 Squadron undertook a reconnaissance trip around the Lens area. The pilots managed to find and attack German road transport in the Arras area. They also attacked ten busses and damaged a large car near Lille. However, the Poles did not have it all their own way. Light anti-aircraft fire was encountered in the Lille area and Flight Lieutenant J. Stasik was hit, baling out into the sea ten miles north of Ostend. A parachute was seen to open and the Air Sea Rescue service was despatched to search the area. Stasik was never found.

Soon the pilots of 303 Squadron were involved in providing escort for the airborne forces involved in Operation *Market Garden*, which began on 17 September 1944. The following day, the squadron lost another pilot when

Right: Warrant Officer Ryszard Gorecki in his Spitfire Mk.VB, possibly W3373. Gorecki survived the war and settled in the USA. (Via P. Sikora)

Flight Sergeant S. Dworski, flying Spitfire MH320, crashed near Roosendaal and was killed. Another of the pilots to become a casualty during this period was Witold A. Herbst.

As it had done on other days during Operation *Market Garden*, the squadron had pre-deployed from Westhampnett to RAF Manston in Kent. It was from there that Herbst and his comrades took off on the 20th: "When we were eventually able to fly in the dirtiest weather imaginable our squadron, like most others, disintegrated into separate quartets in the muck and intense ground fire. After some 30 minutes I decided to get out of there and turned with my section north west.

"Flying home I was careless enough to fly at 5-6 thousand feet over Oostende, still occupied by the *Wehrmacht*. Once again I found out how good the flak was. I was hit but managed to turn back so as to be over our forced around Ostend. I judged that my engine may blow up or catch fire so I parted company with my aircraft [MA795] and landed on Flemish soil."[7]

Herbst landed safely behind Allied lines and soon returned to his unit. As for 303 Squadron, having been involved in intense operations since its arrival at Westhampnett, it was moved north at the end of September 1944, heading for RAF Coltishall.

Whilst 303 Squadron had been in residence at Westhampnett it was joined, on 4 July 1944, by the men and machines of 350 (Belgian) Squadron. Equipped with Spitfire Mk.Vs (which were replaced by Mk.IXs), the Belgians arrived from RAF Friston in East Sussex. They quickly settled in to Westhampnett, the officers being mostly accommodated in Woodcote Farm.

The commanding officer of 350 (Belgian) Squadron at this time was Squadron Leader Baron Michael Donnet DFC, who had escaped from Belgium after the German invasion in a Stampe SV4 two-seater trainer. The aircraft had been de-commissioned by the Germans and he had to

Opposite: The Belgian Prime Minister, Hubert Pierlot, stands in the cockpit of a 350 (Belgian) Squadron Spitfire during his visit to Westhampnett in the summer of 1944. This picture was taken on the airfield's northern boundary. (Via Serge Bonge, 'Belgians in the RAF and SAAF 1940-1945')

Above: Squadron Leader Baron Michael Donnet of 350 (Belgian) Squadron shows the Belgian Prime Minister, Hubert Pierlot, around his unit's Spitfires at Westhampnett on 19 July 1944. (Via Serge Bonge, 'Belgians in the RAF and SAAF 1940-1945')

make up an improvised instrument panel in order to fly it across the Channel.

Donnet recalled his arrival and time at Westhampnett: "On our arrival at Westhampnett on the 4th July … we found nineteen Spitfire Mk.IXs waiting for us, of which three were brand new aircraft. This was a pleasant surprise.

"On the first day I did an air test … after this date the squadron was on operations again over Normandy … During its stay at Westhampnett the squadron carried out over twenty offensive operations. These consisted mainly of fighter sweeps, bomber escorts and heavy bomber escorts. We were operating in daylight against targets at Caen, Falaise and other German defences. I led practically every operation.

"On the 19th July 1944 we had a visit from the Belgian Prime Minister, Mr Pierlot, escorted by a number of personalities. They stayed for lunch with the pilots on the airfield.

"On the 21st July, which was our national day, an attack was planned against buildings used by the German authorities in Brussels, but it was cancelled at the last moment. The Prime Minister did feel that there may have been Belgian civilian casualties.

"On the 24th July, we were flying close escort to aircraft bombing the Falaise Gap, rapidly narrowing the German armies trapped in the pocket. 349 were low cover and we were on top. Suddenly the *Luftwaffe* appeared in the shape of about a dozen Me 109s which came out of the sun, down on to the bombers. 349 got itself engaged in sorting them out whilst we put ourselves in a good position for an attack.

"The squadron stayed until 8 August 1944 when it left for RAF Hawkinge to be re-equipped Spitfire Mk.XIVs and with a role change to intercepting and chasing V-1 flying bombs."[8]

Whilst 350 Squadron was based at Westhampnett, 349 (Belgian) Squadron was stationed nearby at Selsey, and then Merston. From signatures and graffiti still visible on the ceiling and walls in the basement

Above: Prime Minister Hubert Pierlot is talked through the controls of a 350 (Belgian) Squadron Spitfire on 19 July 1944. The squadron had only recently arrived from RAF Friston. The Mk.Vs they flew at the time were soon replaced by the Mk.IX. (Via Serge Bonge, 'Belgians in the RAF and SAAF 1940-1945')

Right: Another view of Prime Minister Hubert Pierlot on the northern boundary of Westhampnett during his tour of the airfield and 350 (Belgian) Squadron in July 1944. (Via Serge Bonge, 'Belgians in the RAF and SAAF 1940-1945')

of Woodcote Farm, it would appear that many opportunities for joint relaxation occurred. A description of some of the graffiti, and one of the social events, has survived in one veteran's diary:

"Flight Sergeant Jean Morel … has worked for days. He has decorated the basement of house where the officers are housed. In the vaults, a skeleton army pursues girls in poses spread over a huge gigantic black and white draught board. Very original and very successful. A house warming party is given. The barrels of beer on the counter in the corner are subject to the test. The Wing Commander is present. Many songs, many shouts and much laughter and good time."[9]

The Belgians departed from Westhampnett on 8 August 1944.

For a month between 2 July and 2 August 1944, Westhampnett was also the home of 501 (County of Gloucester) Squadron, which was equipped with the Hawker Tempest Mk.V. Also leaving in August that year, the squadron was predominately involved in intercepting V-1 flying bombs.

In November 1944, No.83 Group Support Unit arrived at Westhampnett, bringing with it a selection of Spitfires, Mustangs and Typhoons. The airfield was then used as a ferry base from which replacement aircraft were flown to units based on the Continent.

John Thompson was one of the pilots involved in bringing in replacement aircraft to the Westhampnett. He had joined the RAF in 1940, and, after a varied career, joined the RAF's 33 Maintenance Unit at Lyneham. It was from here he was asked to deliver Spitfires to Westhampnett:

"My first visit was on 2 January 1945 when I was ferrying a Spitfire Mk.XIV, NH691. The *Luftwaffe* had made one of their last mass raids on RAF bases in Belgium and Holland on the 1st January and had demolished a large number of our fighter aircraft. An order had gone out to various Maintenance Units to despatch replacement aircraft asap.[10]

Above: Some of 350 (Belgian) Squadron's pilots relax in-between sorties in the walled rear garden of Woodcote Farm. (Via Serge Bonge, 'Belgians in the RAF and SAAF 1940-1945')

"At Lyneham we were instructed to send 3 aircraft to Westhampnett for onward delivery to Brussels by the pilots if no ferry pilots were waiting at Westhampnett. Unfortunately the weather was bad with heavy snow showers topping up the 4 inches of snow that had fallen overnight.

"Eventually we were able to get away in reasonable visibility and low cloud base and made our way to Westhampnett. The airfield was covered in about 4 inches of snow but a runway had been cleared east to west at the north end of the field where the flight huts were then located just beside the Lavant road."

This flight, however, almost ended in disaster, as Thompson goes on to

Above left: Wing Commander Don Kingaby DSO, AFC, DFM and Two Bars, seen here on the left, with Squadron Leader Baron Michael Donnet (centre) and the Belgian Prime Minister, Hubert Pierlot, during the latter's visit to Westhampnett on 19 July 1944. (Via Serge Bonge, 'Belgians in the RAF and SAAF 1940-1945')

Above: A group of 350 (Belgian) Squadron pilots pose for the camera in front of a Mk.IX Spitfire parked on Westhampnett's eastern boundary. This picture was taken near what is today the main entrance to the airfield. (Via Serge Bonge, 'Belgians in the RAF and SAAF 1940-1945')

Above and opposite: Prime Minister Hubert Pierlot addresses personnel from 350 (Belgian) Squadron at Westhampnett on 19 July 1944. The blister hangar in the background was located close to the eastern boundary. (Via Serge Bonge, 'Belgians in the RAF and SAAF 1940-1945')

recall: "Two of us landed and parked near the huts but the third member of the flight, who had been based at Tangmere previously, decided to beat up Tangmere before landing and on returning he landed straight in downwind. The CO of the local squadron had decided to take off at the other end of the strip at the same time as our pilot landed short at the other end. By some miracle and a light fuel load the CO got airborne just in time to pass over the other aircraft. Needless to say he did a very tight circuit and landed to tear our pilot off the most almighty strip!"

This eventful ferry flight was not Thompson's only trip to Westhampnett. "My next visit was on 8 July 1945 in a Miles Falcon which we used for communications at Westland's Aircraft when I was a test pilot there and had a friend who was a Naval officer at the FAA unit on the airfield and who could give me a lift home and back the following morning."[11]

By this stage of the war, Westhampnett had changed beyond all recognition from the RAF's arrival back in the dark days of 1940. By 1945 it had become a fully-fledged fighter station. However, with the fighting in Europe having moved far into Germany, the airfield was put on to a care and maintenance basis in February 1945.

Further change came on 1 March 1945, when Westhampnett was transferred to the Air Staff SHAEF (Supreme Headquarters Allied Expeditionary Force) and used to accommodate elements of one of the RAF's Air Disarmament Wings.

During July the same year the airfield witnessed the arrival of an unusual and varied mix of aircraft – such as Fairey Barracudas, Grumman Avengers and twin-engine Grumman Tigercats – as the Central Fighter Establishment, Naval Air Fighting Development Unit, 787 Naval Air Squadron and other Central Fighter Establishment staff moved in from Tangmere and Ford.

This re-birth did not last long and the airfield fell silent once again at the end of May 1946 – but not forever!

During its active wartime years, Westhampnett saw hundreds of young pilots and groundcrew pass through, many of whom did not return from operations having made the ultimate sacrifice. The airfield had resounded to the dialects of various nations, many far from their homes, and resonated to the throb of Merlins and other aero engines. The airfield had

played a major part in the air battles across the European Theatre of operations, becoming an important RAF fighter station.

Today Westhampnett, or Goodwood as it is now known, is still home to Spitfires and is a thriving general aviation airfield. Often Spitfires of the Boultbee Flight Academy can be seen performing formation take-offs, all of which helps to ensure that one airfield's role in the Second World War is remembered.

Below: Some of 350 (Belgian) Squadron's groundcrew form up by the perimeter track (now the Lavant Straight) to be addressed by Prime Minister Hubert Pierlot. (Via Serge Bonge, 'Belgians in the RAF and SAAF 1940-1945')

Opposite: Belgian Prime Minister Hubert Pierlot during his inspection of Westhampnett. The building seen here was located on the eastern boundary. (Via Serge Bonge, 'Belgians in the RAF and SAAF 1940-1945')

Above: During his visit to Westhampnett on 19 July 1944, Prime Minister Hubert Pierlot was accompanied by Air Commodore Louis Wouters, who commanded all of the Belgians serving in the RAF, and Wing Commander Lucien Leboutte DFC. The latter had previously flown Bristol Beaufighters with 141 Squadron from Ford. (Via Serge Bonge, 'Belgians in the RAF and SAAF 1940-1945')

Above: Pilots from 350 (Belgian) Squadron pictured in the garden at Woodcote Farm whilst relaxing between sorties in July 1944. They are, from the rear forwards, as follows: Flying Officer Fifi Veerporten; Squadron Leader Baron Michael Donnet; Flying Officer J. Wustefeld; Flight Lieutenant H. Smets; Flying Officer R. Duchateu; G. Beckers; Flight Lieutenant P. Siroux; Flight Lieutenant R. Muls; and Flight Lieutenant Lucien Lelarge. As Lelarge was posted to 349 (Belgian) Squadron on 21 July 1944, we know that this photograph was taken prior to that date. (Via Serge Bonge, 'Belgians in the RAF and SAAF 1940-1945')

Opposite: Some of 350 (Belgian) Squadron's pilots resting in front of a recently-delivered Spitfire Mk.IX. Note the long range fuel tank mounted under the centre of the fuselage. (Via Serge Bonge, 'Belgians in the RAF and SAAF 1940-1945')

Opposite: A Spitfire Mk.IX of 350 (Belgian) Squadron at Westhampnett. Coded 'MN-Z' and with the serial number ML137, this aircraft was flown by Flight Lieutenant G. de Patoul, who is seen here with his groundcrew. (Via Serge Bonge, 'Belgians in the RAF and SAAF 1940-1945')

Above: Another view of groundcrew with Flight Lieutenant G. de Patoul's Spitfire, ML137. This aircraft had been delivered to the squadron by 46 Maintenance Unit and was reported as being on its strength from 9 July 1944. (Via Serge Bonge, 'Belgians in the RAF and SAAF 1940-1945')

Right: A final shot of ML137. Flight Lieutenant G. de Patoul was rested from operations on 31 July 1944, whilst ML137 was eventually transferred to 322 (Dutch) Squadron. (Via Serge Bonge, 'Belgians in the RAF and SAAF 1940-1945')

Opposite: A view of the southern side of the Officers' Mess at Westhampnett, the main building of Woodcote Farm, as pictured by a pilot from 350 (Belgian) Squadron. The cellar of this building was used by the squadron as a bar area and to this day the ceiling and walls are covered in the signatures and graffiti of men from 350 (Belgian) Squadron, its sister unit, 349 (Belgian) Squadron, as well as a few from 303 (Polish) Squadron. Note the formation of 350 Squadron Spitfires above the chimney. (Via Serge Bonge, 'Belgians in the RAF and SAAF 1940-1945')

Below: Squadron Leader Baron Michael Donnet and other 350 (Belgian)

Squadron personnel dining in Woodcote Farmhouse. (Via Serge Bonge, 'Belgians in the RAF and SAAF 1940-1945')

Below: Whilst the Belgian squadrons were still in residence at Westhampnett they were joined by the men and machines of 501 (County of Gloucester) Squadron. Equipped with the Tempest Mk.V, 501 Squadron was tasked with undertaking *Diver* patrols in an attempt to intercept V-1 flying bombs. It left in August 1944, being replaced by Nos. 118 and 124 squadrons, with both units operating the Spitfire Mk.IX. (Key Collection)

Left: Despite its poor quality, this image shows the flypast undertaken by 350 (Belgian) Squadron on the occasion of Prime Minister Hubert Pierlot's visit to Westhampnett on 19 July 1944. (Via Serge Bonge, 'Belgians in the RAF and SAAF 1940-1945')

Right: An aerial view of Westhampnett taken in 1946. This image shows the extent of the development of the RAF airfield since its humble beginnings in 1940. Note that a T2 hangar is clearly visible on the boundary and how the runway extension constructed in the south-east corner to accommodate Typhoons runs into the adjacent fields. The airfield also occupied other sites in the area, including in the village of Westerton. The airfield map shows that by 1946 there were 307 buildings associated with RAF Westhampnett. (English Heritage; NMR)

APPENDIX
THE WESTHAMPNETT SQUADRONS

Squadron	Aircraft	Codes	Duties	Dates
145	Hurricane I	SO	Fighter Defence	23 July 1940 to 14 August 1940
602 (City of Glasgow)	Spitfire I	LO	Fighter Defence	14 August 1940 to 17 December 1940
302 (Polish)	Hurricane I	WX	Coastal patrols, Circuses	23 November 1940 to 6 April 1940
610 (County of Chester)	Spitfire I, IIa and Vb	DW	Circuses, Rangers, Rhubarbs	19 December 1940 to 27 August 1941
616 (South Yorkshire)	Spitfire IIa, IIb and Vb	YQ	Circuses, Rangers, Rhubarbs	9 May 1941 to 5 October 1941
129 (Mysore)	Spitfire Vb and Vc	DV	Circuses, Rangers, Rhubarbs	29 August 1941 to 29 July 1942
65 (East India)	Spitfire Vb and Vc	YT	Circuses, Rangers, Rhubarbs	7 October 1941 to 21 December 1941
41	Spitfire Vb	EB	Circuses, Rangers, Rhubarbs	16 December 1941 to 31 March 1942
340 (Île-de-France)	Spitfire Vb	GW	Circuses, Rangers, Rhubarbs	7 April 1941 to 28 July 42
56 (Punjab)	Typhoon Ib	US	Patrols	30 May 1942 to 7 June 1942
416 (City of Oshawa) RCAF	Spitfire Vb	DN	Circuses, Rangers, Rhubarbs	25 June 1942 to 8 July 1942
309th USAAF	Spitfire Vb	WZ	Convoy escort, Rodeos, patrols	30 July 1942 to 30 September 1942
308th USAAF	Spitfire Vb	HL	Convoy escort, Rodeos, patrols	29 August 1942 to 30 September 1942
48th/49th USAAF	P38	ES/QU	Operational experience	1 October 1942 to 15 October 1942
616 (South Yorkshire)	Spitfire VI	YQ	Circuses, Rangers, Rhubarbs	29 October 1942 to 1 January 1943
124 (Baroda)	Spitfire VI	ON	Circuses, Rangers, Rhubarbs	29 October 1942 to 6 November 1942
131 (County of Kent)	Spitfire Vb and Vc	NX	Circuses, Rangers, Rhubarbs	7 November 1942 to 22 January 1943
485 (NZ)	Spitfire Vb	OU	Circuses, Rangers, Rhubarbs	2 January 1943 to 15 February 1943
610 (County of Chester)	Spitfire Vb and Vc	DW	Circuses, Rangers, Rhubarbs	20 January 1943 to 29 April 1943
485 (NZ)	Spitfire Vb	OU	Circuses, Rangers, Rhubarbs	22 February 1943 to 30 June 1943
501 (County of Gloucester)	Spitfire Vb	SD	Circuses, Rangers, Rhubarbs	21 April 1943 to 21 June 1943
167	Spifire Vb and Vc	VL	Circuses, Rangers, Rhubarbs	21 May 1943 to June 1943
41	Spitfire XII	EB	Circuses, Rangers, Rhubarbs	19 June 1943 to 4 October 1943
91 (Nigeria)	Spitfire XII	DL	Circuses, Rangers, Rhubarbs	28 June 1943 to 3 October 1943
118	Spitfire Vb	NK	Circuses, Rangers, Rhubarbs	15 August 1943 to 23 August 1943

Squadron	Aircraft	Codes	Duties	Dates
175	Typhoon Ib	HH	Roadsteads, Ramrods, Noballs	9 October 1943 to 24 February 1944
174	Typhoon Ib	XP	Roadsteads, Ramrods, Noballs	10 October 1943 to 21 January 1944
245 (Northern Rhodesia)	Typhoon Ib	MR	Roadsteads, Ramrods, Noballs	10 October 1943 to 1 April 1944
174	Typhoon Ib	XP	Roadsteads, Ramrods, Noballs	4 February 1944 to 1 April 1944
175	Typhoon Ib	HH	Roadsteads, Ramrods, Noballs	8 March 1944 to 1 April 1944
168	Mustang I (detachment)	QC	Photographic reconnaissance	22 March 1944 to 25 March 1944
441 (Silver Fox) RCAF	Spitfire IX	9G	Circuses	1 April 1944 to 12 April 1944
442 (Caribou) RCAF	Spitfire IX	Y2	Circuses	1 April 1944 to 22 April 1944
443 (Hornet) RCAF	Spitfire IX	2I	Circuses, high level fighter cover	1 April 1944 to 22 April 1944
184	Typhoon 1b	BR	Roadsteads, Ramrods, Noballs	23 April 1944 to 13 May 1944
303 (Polish)	Spitfire IX	RF	Roadsteads, Ramrods, Noballs	18 June 1944 to 26 June 1944
130 (Punjab)	Spitfire Vb, Vc	AP	Circus, beachhead patrols	19 June 1944 to 26 June1944
402 (City of Winnipeg)	Spitfire Vc	AE	Circus, beachhead patrols	19 June 1944 to 27 June 1944
41	Spitfire XII	EB	Anti-flying bomb	27 June 1944 to 2 July 1944
610 (County of Chester)	Spitfire XIV	DW	Anti-flying bomb	27 June 1944 to 2 July 1944
501 (County of Gloucester)	Tempest V	SD	Anti-flying bomb	2 July 1944 to 2 August 1944
350 (Belgian)	Spitfire IX	MN	Circuses, beachhead patrols	4 July 1944 to 8 August 1944
303 (Polish)	Spitfire IX	RF	Circuses, escort	9 August 1944 to 25 September 1944
118	Spitfire IX	NK	Circuses, escort	29 August 1944 to 24 September 1944
124 (Baroda)	Spitfire IX	ON	Circuses, escort	9 August 1944 to 22 February 1945
83 GSU*	Spitfires, Mustangs etc.	No code	Replacement aircraft	3 November 1944 to 22 February 1945
CFE**, 787 NAS***	Barracudas, Avengers	YD	Combat tactics	13 July 1945 to 27 November 1945

GSU stands for Group Support Unit
**CFE stands for Central Fighter Establishment*
***NAS stands for Naval Air Squadron*

REFERENCES AND NOTES

Chapter 1: In the Beginning

1. The publication referred to here is Hillier, M., Sinanan, D., and Percival, G., *Westhampnett at War* (Yellowman, 2010).

Chapter 2: The Battle of Britain

1. TNA, AIR 27/984, 145 Squadron's Operations Record Book.
2. Norman L.R. Franks, *Royal Air Force Fighter Command Losses of the Second World War*, Volume 1 (Midland Publishing, Hersham, 2008), p.45.
3. IWM Sound Archive 13265, recording of interview with Eric Marsden.
4. *Ibid.*
5. IWM Sound Archive 13152, recording of interview with Peter Lawrence Parrott.
6. IWM Sound Archive 13265.
7. IWM Sound Archive 13152.
8. Air Vice-Marshal Sandy Johnstone CB, DFC, *Enemy in the Sky: My 1940 Diary* (William Kimber, London, 1976), p.94.
9. F.G. Nancarrow, *Glasgow's Fighter Squadron* (Collins, London, 1942), p.45.
10. Air Vice-Marshal Sandy Johnstone CB, DFC, *ibid.*
11. F.G. Nancarrow, *ibid.*
12. *Ibid*, pp.45-6.
13. Jeffery Quill, *Spitfire: A Test Pilot's Story* (Crecy Publishing, Manchester, 1998), p.182-3.
14. Sandy Johnstone recalls that the squadron's officers and men used several pubs in the local area, including the Old Ship Inn at Bosham. Other accounts mention pubs in and around Chichester such as The Unicorn, Rose and Crown and the Dolphin and Anchor.
15. Letters from Nigel Rose to the author.

Chapter 3: On to the Offensive

1. For more information on the despatch, see John Grehan and Martin Mace, *Defending Britain's Skies 1940-1945* (Pen & Sword, Barnsley, 2014).
2. TNA, AIR 50/116.
3. Archives of the 610 (County of Chester) Squadron Association.
4. Denchfield recalled the following regarding the history of his aircraft: "DW-P (N3249) was manufactured by Vickers Supermarine at Woolston near Portsmouth in December 1939, being in one of the earliest batches made. She had flown with 92 and 602 Squadrons; with 92 she had scored over France during the Dunkirk evacuation in the hands of Robert Stanford Tuck."
5. Account by Herbert David Denchfield, correspondence with author.
6. Stewart Wilson, *Almost Unknown, The Story of Squadron Leader Tony Gaze OAM, DFC*** (Chevron Publishing Group, Lane Cove, 2009), p.24.
7. TNA, AIR 27/2126/29.
8. The late Sir Alan Smith DFC & Bar, an interview with the author.
9. *Ibid.*
10. Johnnie Johnson, *Wing Leader* (Chatto and Windus, London, 1956), p.85.
11. *Ibid.*
12. The late Sir Alan Smith DFC & Bar, an interview with the author.
13. *Ibid.*

Chapter 4: The Channel Dash and The Dieppe Raid

1. Armitage was shot down on a Wing escort over France in September 1941. He survived to become a prisoner of war.
2. Flight Lieutenant Ray Sherk, correspondence with author.
3. Family archives, via Bill Whalen.

4. Waghorn was never found and he is commemorated on Panel 54 of the Runnymede Memorial.
5. Flight Lieutenant Ray Sherk, correspondence with author.
6. TNA, AIR 27/934.
7. Wing Commander Bob Middlemiss, correspondence with author.
8. *Ibid.*
9. This squadron is also referred to in many accounts as 340 (Free French) Squadron.
10. Jenks, interview with author.
11. Throughout June 1942, 129 Squadron is listed as having undertaken 824 hours of flying with only three accidents.
12. TNA AIR 27/934/23; TNA AIR 27/934/24.
13. TNA AIR /27/624/69.
14. Oxspring, Group Captain Bobby, *Spitfire Command* (William Kimber, 1984), p.113-4.
15. TNA AIR 27/934/23; TNA AIR 27/934/24.
16. Anderson, Captain Barry J. USAF, *Army Air Forces Stations: The Stations Where U.S. Army Air Forces Personnel Served in the United Kingdom During World War II*, a report for the USAF Historical Research Center, January 1985.
17. The 307th Fighter Squadron took up residence at RAF Biggin Hill; the 308th Fighter Squadron at RAF Kenley.
18. Here Strawn is referring to Colonel John R. 'Shorty' Hawkins, who had been responsible for forming the three squadrons of the 31st Fighter Group at Baer Field in the USA in January 1942.
19. Hillier, Mark, Percival, Gregory, and Sinanan, Dieter, *To War in A Spitfire* (Yellowman 2012), p.45-81.
20. *Ibid.*
21. Squadron Leader Doug Brown, correspondence with author.
22. Hodgkinson, Colin, *Best Foot Forward* (Corgi, London, 1978), pp.145-6.
23. Peter Graham, *Skypilot; Memoirs from Take-Off to Landing* (Pentland Books, 2001).

Chapter 5: Typhoons and the Amiens Raid
1. Davidson had been a pre-war pilot who served in the Middle East, Greece and then with 30 Squadron in the North African campaign before being posted to Ceylon to fight against the Japanese.
2. Flight Sergeant Bill Waudby survived, evaded capture and eventually made a 'home run'. It was in March 1944 that Bill reached the Pyrenees, reportedly crossing into Spain with a group of sixty-two evaders. One of the group, Bill Furniss-Roe, recalled how the escapers, having reached Spanish soil, met the British Consul before travelling on by taxi – albeit with a stop at Zaragossa airfield where they were entertained by the Spanish Air Force and closely inspected their Messerschmitt Bf 109s.
3. Frank Wheeler, correspondence with author.

Chapter 6: D-Day and Beyond
1. Frank 'Dutch' Holland, with Adam Wilkins, *D-Day Plus one: Shot Down and on the Run in France* (Grub Street, London, 2009), pp.108-9.
2. *Ibid*, p.109.
3. Evan Bumford, *At His Majesty's Expense* (privately published).
4. Squadron Leader Doug Brown, correspondence with author.
5. Witold A. Herbst, correspondence with author.
6. *Ibid.*
7. *Ibid.*
8. Baron M. Donnet, correspondence with author.
9. Via Serge Bonge, author of the excellent *Belgians in the RAF and SAAF 1940-1945* website: www.350sqn.be
10. The *Luftwaffe* attack referred to here by John Thompson was Operation *Bodenplatte* ('Baseplate'), this being an attempt by the Germans to cripple the Allied air forces in the Low Countries during their Ardennes offensive.
11. John Thompson, correspondence with author.

SELECTED BIBLIOGRAPHY AND SOURCE INFORMATION

BOOKS

Allen, H.R., *Battle For Britain, The Recollections of Wing Commander H.R. 'Dizzy' Allen* (Corgi, 1975).

____, *Who Won the Battle of Britain?* (Harper Collins, 1976).

Austin, A.B., *Fighter Command* (Victor Gollanz Ltd, 1941).

Barthrop, Paddy, *Paddy, The Life and Times of Wing Commander Patrick Barthropp* (J&KHP, 2001).

Bishop, Patrick, *Fighter Boys: Saving Britain 1940* (Harper Collins, 2004).

Brew, Steve, *Blood Sweat and Valour, 41 Squadron RAF 1942-1945* (Fonthill Media, 2012).

Brickhill, Paul, *Reach For the Sky: The Story ogf Douglas Bader CBE, DSO, DFC* (Collins, 1962).

Brooks, Robin J., *Sussex Airfield in the Second World War*, (Countryside Books, 1993).

Brown, Hamish, *Wine Women and Song, A Spitfire Pilot's Story* (Stayer, 2011).

Burns, Michael G., *Bader: The Man and His Men* (Cassell, 1998).

Byron, Reginald, and Coxon, David, *Tangmere, Famous Royal Air Force Fighter Station: An Authorised History* (Grub Street, 2013).

Caldwell, Donald L., *JG26: Top Guns of the Luftwaffe* (Orion Books, 1991).

Delve, Ken, and Pitchfork, Graham, *South Yorkshire's Own, The story of 616 Squadron* (Doncaster Books, 1990).

Dundas, Hugh, *Flying Start* (Stanley Paul, 1989).

Donnet, M. *Flight to Freedom* (Ian Allen, 1974).

Franks, Norman L.R., *Royal Air Force Fighter Command Losses of the Second World War, Volume 1* (Midland Publishing, 1997).

____, *Royal Air Force Fighter Command Losses of the Second World War, Volume 2* (Midland Publishing, 1998).

____, *Royal Air Force Fighter Command Losses of the Second World War, Volume 3* (Midland Publishing, 2000).

Gelb, Norman, *Scramble* (Pan, 1986).

Golley, John, *The Day of the Typhoon, Flying with the Royal Air Force Tankbusters in Normandy* (Patrick Stephens, 1986).

Graham, Peter, *Skypilot; Memoirs from Take-Off to Landing* (Pentland Books, 2001).

Hillier, Mark, Percival, Gregory, and Sinanan, Dieter, *To War in A Spitfire* (Yellowman 2012).

____, *Westhampnett at War* (Yellowman, 2010).

Hodgkinson, Colin, *Best Foot Forward* (Odhams Press, 1957).

Holland, Frank 'Dutch', *D-Day Plus One: Shot Down and on the Run in France* (Grub Street, 2009).

Hough, Richard, and Richards, Denis, *The Battle of Britain, the Jubilee History* (Hodder & Stoughton, 1990).

Houlton, Jonnie, *Spitfire Strikes* (John Murray, 1985).

Jackson, Robert, *Douglas Bader* (Arthur Baker, 1983).

Johnstone, Air Vice-Marshal Sandy, CB, DFC, *Adventure in the Sky* (William Kimber, 1978).

____, *Enemy in the Sky, My 1940 Diary* (William Kimber, 1979).

____, *Spitfire in to War* (William Kimber, 1986).

____, *Diary of an Aviator* (Airlife, 1993).

Johnson, Johnnie, *Wing Leader* (Chatto & Windus, 1956).

Kent, Captain Johnny, *One of the Few* (Cerberus Publishing, 1971).

Kucera, Dennis C., *In a Now Forgotten Sky – The 31st FG in WW2* (Flying Machines Press, 1997).

Lelliot, Graham, *A German Bomber on Worthing Soil* (privately published, 2007).

Levine, Joshua, *Forgotten Voices of the Blitz and the Battle For Britain: A New History in the Words of the Men and Women on Both Sides* (Ebury Press, 2006).

Lucas, Laddie, *Flying Colours* (Stanley Paul, 1981).

McRoberts, *Lions Rampant, The Story of 602 Spitfire Squadron* (William Kimber, 1985).

Mouchotte, Rene, *The Mouchotte Diaries 1940-1943* (Staples, 1956).

Nancarrow, F.G., *Glasgow's Fighter Squadron* (Collins, 1942).

Olson, Lynne and Cloud, Stanley, *For Your Freedom and Ours: The Kosciuszko Squadron – Forgotten Heroes of World War II* (William Heineman, 2003).

Oxspring, Group Captain Bobby, *Spitfire Command* (William Kimber, 1984).

Pitchfork, Graham, *The RAF's First Jet Squadron: 616 (South Yorkshire)* (The History Press, 2009).

Robinson, Anthony, *RAF Fighter Squadrons in the Battle of Britain* (Weidenfeld & Nicholson, 1987).

Roddis, Joe, *In Support of the Few* (Yellowman, 2013).

Rowland, David, *Spitfires Over Sussex* (Finsbury Publishing, 2000).

Sarkar, Dilip, *Bader's Tangmere Spitfires: The Untold Story* (Patrick Stephens, 1996).

Saunders, Andy, *Bader's Last Flight: An In-Depth Investigation of a Great WWII Mystery* (Grub Street, 2007).

Shores, Christopher, and Williams, Clive, *Aces High* (Grub Street, 1999).

Thomas, Chris, and Shores, Christopher, *2nd Tactical Air Force, Vol. 2: Breakout to Bodenplatte, July 1944 to January 1945* (Ian Allen, 2009).

Townsend, Peter, *Duel In the Dark* (Arrow, 1988).

Wellum, G. *First Light* (Penguin Viking, 2002).

Wilson, Stewart, *Almost Unknown, The Story of Squadron Leader Tony Gaze OAM DFC** Australian Spitfire Ace and Racing Driver* (Chevron Publishing, 2009).

Wynn, Kenneth G., *Men of the Battle of Britain* (CCB Associates, 1999).

Zamoyski, Adam, *The Forgotten Few: The Polish Air Force in World War II* (Pen and Sword, 2004).

THE NATIONAL ARCHIVES

AIR 50/428, 175 Squadron Operations Record Book.

AIR 27/934, 129 Squadron Operations Record Book.

AIR 27/984, 145 Squadron Operations Record Book.

AIR 27/2074, 602 Squadron Operations Record Book.

AIR 27/2106, 610 Squadron Operations Record Book.

AIR 27/2126, 616 Squadron Operations Record Book.

PRIVATE RECORDS

Anderson, Flying Officer John (610 Squadron).

Brewer, Sergeant R. L. (616 Squadron).

Denchfield, Warrant Officer David (610 Squadron).

Herbst, Flying Officer W. (303 Squadron).

Middlemiss, Wing Commander Bob (41 Squadron).

Smith, Flight Lieutenant Sir Alan (616 Squadron).

PERSONAL CORRESPONDENCE

Anderson, Flying Officer John (610 Squadron).

Brown, Squadron Leader Doug (485 Squadron).

Denchfield Warrant Officer David (610 Squadron).

Donnett, Wing Commander Baron M. DFC (350 Squadron).

Ellis, Mary (Air Transport Auxiliary).

Graham, Sergeant Peter (41 Squadron).

Herbst, Flying Officer, W. (303 Squadron).

Hodges, Warrant Officer W. (174 Squadron).

Rose, Pilot Officer Nigel (602 Squadron).

Reeves, Flight Lieutenant Richard (129 Squadron).

Sherk, Flight Lieutenant Ray (129 Squadron).

Smith, Flight Lieutenant Sir Alan DFC & Bar (616 Squadron).

Thompson, John (Spitfire Test Pilot).

Wheeler, Flying Officer Frank DFC (174 Squadron).

WEBSITES

www.31stfightergroup.com

www.cieldegloire.com

www.350sqn.be

http://brew.clients.ch/RAF41Sqdn.htm

www.610squadron.com

INDEXES

Note: Entries in italics indicate a reference to a caption.